Men-at-Arms • 247

Romano-Byzantine Armies 4th–9th Centuries

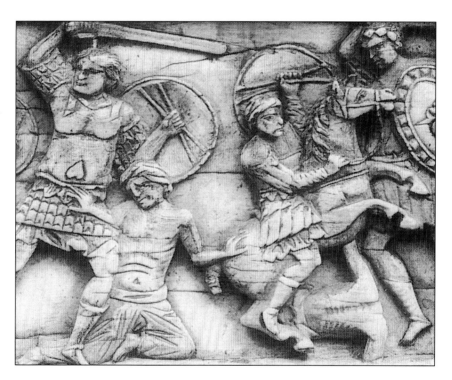

David Nicolle · Illustrated by Angus McBride

Series editor Martin Windrow

MW01156714

First published in Great Britain in 1992 by Osprey Publishing,
Midland House, West Way, Botley, Oxford OX2 0PH, UK
44-02 23rd St, Suite 219, Long Island City, NY 11101, USA
Email: info@ospreypublishing.com

Osprey Publishing is part of the Osprey Group.

© 1992 Osprey Publishing Ltd.

All rights reserved. Apart from any fair dealing for the purpose of private study, research,
criticism or review, as permitted under the Copyright, Designs and Patents Act, 1988,
no part of this publication may be reproduced, stored in a retrieval system, or transmitted
in any form or by any means, electronic, electrical, chemical, mechanical, optical,
photocopying, recording or otherwise, without the prior written permission of the
copyright owner. Enquiries should be addressed to the Publishers.

Transferred to digital print on demand 2010

First published 1992
14th impression 2008

Printed and bound by Cadmus Communications, USA

A CIP catalogue record for this book is available from the British Library

ISBN: 978 1 85532 224 0

Series Editor: Martin Windrow
Filmset in Great Britain

Dedication
For Gina Hazell
Italy, my Italy!
Queen Mary's saying serves for me –
(When fortune's malice
Lost her – Calais) –
Open my heart and you will see
Graved inside of it, 'Italy.'
                    (Robert Browning)

Artist's note
Readers may care to note that the original paintings from which the colour plates in this
book were prepared are available for private sale. All reproduction copyright whatsoever
is retained by the Publishers. All enquiries should be addressed to:

Scorpio Gallery
PO Box 475
Hailsham
E. Sussex
BN27 2SL

The Publishers regret that they can enter into no correspondence upon this matter.

The Woodland Trust
Osprey Publishing is supporting the Woodland Trust, the UK's leading woodland
conservation charity, by funding the dedication of trees.

www.ospreypublishing.com

INTRODUCTION

The Fall of the Roman Empire has been explained in economic, moral and even racial terms, but the facts of military collapse are easier to chart. Roman frontiers were often artificial; for while forests and mountains formed real barriers, rivers were more a means of communication than an obstacle. The Rhine and Danube had for centuries marked the limit of Roman rule, but behind them – apart from the Alps which protected Italy – there were few effective barriers. Most Roman *limes* or frontiers consisted of zones rather than lines, and here peoples met rather than being separated.

In general the Eastern half of the Roman Empire was, by the mid-4th century AD, economically stronger than the West, and there was no real evidence to indicate that Eastern 'Greek' soldiers were inferior to Western 'Roman' soldiers. Various military reforms had, however, been based upon Hellenistic Greek rather than Roman concepts, and also reflected Germanic or Iranian influences from beyond the frontier. Meanwhile the military importance of frontier peoples grew. Nor should the fact that half the Roman Empire fell to barbarian assault hide the remarkable effectiveness of this late Roman defence structure, given the weakened foundations on which it was built. A water-tight frontier was now impossible, so the late Roman army relied on a screen of garrisons backed up by mobile field armies. Garrisons were to hold minor enemy incursions and, by forcing an invader to disperse in search of food, they also made him vulnerable to counterattack by the nearest field army.

The weakness of this system lay in the slow speed even of field armies, which also had to be spread over a wide area decreasing the Emperor's control. The Roman army also failed to achieve a decisive superiority in cavalry, while troops tied down in static garrison duties declined in quality. Meanwhile late Roman Emperors generally owed their position to the army; power often lay in the hands of competing generals, while civil wars were more of a threat to ordinary people than were foreign invasions.

The Byzantine Empire was, of course, merely the Eastern part of the old Roman Empire under a new name – the disappearance of the Western half in the 5th century generally being regarded as the moment of transition. Though deeply Christian, Byzantium was very militarized and as cruel as any of its foes, with religious strife being almost as common as religious debate. The Sassanian invasions of the early 7th century were also very destructive. For a generation Byzantium lost Egypt, Syria and eastern Anatolia. Many cities were destroyed, the overall population of what is now Turkey declining for another five hundred years until the Turkish conquest led to a revival.

Although the Byzantine Empire was a continuation of the Roman Empire and faced similar military problems, its solutions were very different. In North Africa, for example, Rome's large army concentrated on securing main roads and urban centres. Byzantium's smaller army built more fortifications and took a defensive stance. The most striking characteristic of later Byzantine military thinking was, however, the *theme* or provincial army system, which owed nothing to ancient Roman tradition. The

Carving of a Roman or allied Arab horseman using a 'horned saddle', perhaps 3rd century. (Local Museum, inv. B, Suwaydah, Syria)

basic character of Roman and Byzantine armies also differed, Rome relying on discipline and drill, Byzantium on strategy and generalship. It has even been suggested that, from the 7th to 12th centuries, there was no 'East' no 'West' in the Mediterranean world. Such a view might be oversimplified, but in purely military terms Western Europe, the Byzantine Empire and the Muslim lands did share a common heritage.

In terms of technology the 5th to 9th centuries were certainly a time of great change. Greek Fire, the 'terror weapon' of the Middle Ages, was probably invented in Egypt towards the end of Byzantine rule and there were also major developments in horse harness, most stemming from Central Asia, with improvements to saddle, bridle, horse-shoes and, most striking of all, the introduction of stirrups. Other changes could be seen in naval tactics, with the ship-disabling beak replacing the ancient ship-sinking ram. Meanwhile Mediterranean shipwrights moved from the old hull-first to the modern frame-first construction system, and the triangular lateen sail was introduced from the Indian Ocean. The hinged stern rudder of Chinese origin may have been known to Muslim sailors in the Indian Ocean by the 9th or 10th centuries, but whether it was used by Mediterranean sailors as yet remains unclear.

Copy of lost wall paintings in the Imperial Chamber at Luxor, celebrating the Emperor Diocletian's military reorganization at the end of the 3rd century. Note the new form of saddle, the large cavalry shield and the shaved military haircut of the soldier on the left. (Ms. G. Wilkinson, Sect. A.XXII, Bodleian Lib., Oxford)

COLLAPSE AND SURVIVAL

The officer corps of the later Roman army was often motivated by political ambition, while the bulk of troops were now recruited from frontier areas, particularly in Germany, as the centre of the Empire became demilitarized. There were increasing problems with conscription, with a huge list of exemptions ranging from bakers to senators. Men mutilated themselves to avoid the call-up, while recruits had to be locked away each night to stop desertion. Pay was inadequate and, despite tax concessions, allocations of derelict land and small cash grants, veterans got less than they had in earlier centuries. Discipline was theoretically harsh but in reality trained troops were so valuable that severe punishments were rarely used. Meanwhile many civilians complained that the Empire pampered its troops. As outlying provinces were lost, however, conscription returned to the centre – including Italy – but here social tensions had undermined patriotic feeling. Yet it was still possible to levy conscripts as late as AD 403.

Not surprisingly, the authorities looked for fighting men wherever they could be found. Iranian-speaking Sarmatian cavalry nomads from the Russian steppes were settled in various parts of the Empire, including Britain, where a unit had been stationed in the Fylde area of northern Lancashire. Goth Germans were more widespread, some even being stationed in Arabia. Following Rome's disastrous defeat by the Visigoths (Western Goths) at Adrianople (mod. Edirne) in AD 378, some low-quality garrison soldiers were drummed into the field army, but were not up to the task. On the other hand indigenous troops successfully fought brigands within their own areas. Instead, the Empire enlisted contingents of barbarian *foederati* under their own leaders instead of recruiting them individually as before. Roman resentment led to at least one massacre of Goths, yet Germans remained a vital element in the army until the 7th century.

The late Roman army differed both in organization and size from earlier armies. *Limitanei* frontier forces now consisted of cavalry *equites*, infantry *milites* and auxiliaries. Units were, however, smaller than the old

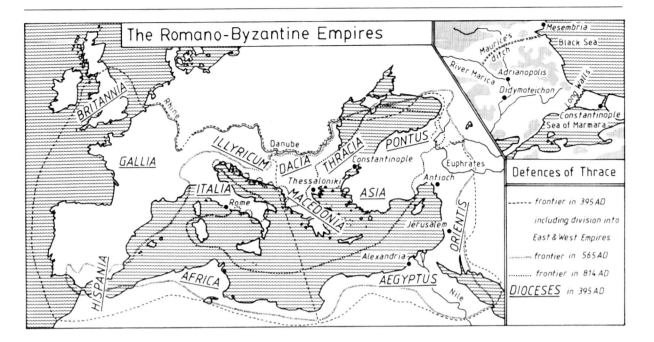

The Romano-Byzantine Empires

Defences of Thrace

- - - - - frontier in 395 AD

including division into

East & West Empires

- - - - frontier in 565 AD

- - - - frontier in 814 AD

DIOCESES in 395 AD

frontier legions and soon integrated into local society. The *comitatenses* field armies were garrisoned in larger cities, while *pseudocomitatenses* seem to have consisted of units withdrawn from the frontier to reinforce a field army.

According to the *Notitia Dignitatum*, written at the end of the 4th century but updated for the Western provinces around AD 430, just under half the army was stationed in the Western part of the Empire, two-thirds of these being frontier troops. By the end of the 4th century up to a sixth of the army had specialist roles, and the *Notitia Dignitatum* shows just where they were stationed. A greater number of mobile forces were based in the West but the majority of heavily armoured *clibanarii* and *cataphracti* cavalry were in the East. *Sagitarii* mounted archers could be found everywhere in frontier and field armies, while infantry archers still outnumbered those on horseback even in field armies. *Lanciarii* infantry spearmen and *ballistarii* catapult operators were all in the East, except for a single unit on the Rhine. One unit of slingers is mentioned in the East. Camel mounted *dromedarrii* were based in Egypt and Palestine, experts in river warfare along the Danube. Elite *exploratores*, *praeventores* and *superventores* scouts and 'commandos' were also mostly in the West.

Command Structure

Constantine (AD 324–337) probably introduced the new senior positions of *Magister Peditem* (Commander of Infantry) and *Magister Equitum* (Commander of Cavalry), but by the end of the 4th century these had been combined as the *Magister Militum*, at least in the Eastern part of the Empire. In reality much authority was delegated to *Comes* and *Dux* field and frontier commanders. Yet a powerful general like Stilicho could still dominate all the Western armies at the end of the 4th century.

After the death of Theodosius I (AD 379–395) the Empire officially split into Eastern and Western halves. The quality of armies declined steeply and defence was gradually delegated to local level; yet military ranks increased in number and complexity. Most *Tribuni* had disappeared with the disbanding of the *Praetorians* by Constantine. Those that remained were now very senior, commanding the Imperial Stables, the *Scholae* guards, some field armies and the staff officers. A kind of staff college also developed in which NCOs were trained for senior regimental command up to the rank of *Tribunus*. Second in command to a *Tribunus* was his *Vicarius*, often with the rank of *Primicerius* or *Domesticus*; below the *Primicerius* was a *Senator*. The *Dux* probably ranked between a *Senator* and a *Centenarius* or Centurion, who now had varied ranks, the chief among them being a *Princeps*.

Around the Emperor were his guards, the *Palatini* who had replaced the old *Praetorians*. Closest and

5

most powerful was the *Comes Domesticorum* or commander of staff officers. *Protectores Domestici* often served as staff officers, and young men of 19 could be commissioned directly in their ranks, while others rose through the ranks before joining the staff around the age of forty.

Quite separate from the Imperial forces were various private armies which sprang up during the Empire's final centuries. Known as *bucellarii*, many were raised by local magnates. They swore oaths of loyalty to their employers instead of the government and, unlike the official *Bucellarii* of regional governors, were regarded as a threat to peace.

Problems and Collapse

The invasions of the late 4th century severely damaged the army's command structure, while the Visigoths' sack of Rome in AD 410 shattered the administration of the Western Empire. There was a modest recovery under Honorius (AD 394–423), largely using the Emperor's Goth mercenaries and a few indigenous troops; but Honorius did not attempt

too much, and made no effort to retake Britain. After his reign, however, the Empire's meagre resources were frequently devoted to putting down usurpers. Despite massive desertions by the often unpaid frontier *limitanii*, archaeology shows that soldiers were now bringing their families within the forts. The quality of the officer corps had clearly declined, with some reportedly stealing their own men's pay. In AD 444 Valentinian III admitted that the taxpayers were exhausted and there was no money to pay his troops. Many Romans deserted to join what looked like the rising empire of Attila, and the Huns were only defeated with help from the equally dangerous Visigoths, the last Roman armies simply withering away. Nevertheless, to the very end plaintive messages came from units of *limitanii* on the Danube frontier begging for back pay until in AD 476, the last Western Emperor was finally deposed by his own Germanic *foederati*.

JUSTINIAN AND HIS SUCCESSORS

By the late 5th century Roman troops were so demoralized that Emperors feared to go to war because a gathering of armies so often led to unrest. The 5th and 6th centuries were, in fact, the worst for military revolts, and many modifications to the command structure aimed at avoiding such trouble. The Eastern Empire often relied on bribery to turn one enemy against another and so defend its shrunken frontiers. However, Justinian I (AD 527–565) reorganized the armies of the East or, as it could now be called, the Byzantine Empire, and regained large parts of what had been the Western Empire.

By Justinian's time the Empire's revived economy allowed it to field a small but highly trained and well-equipped army. *Foederati* units now included both barbarian volunteers and indigenous Roman troops rather than consisting of barbarians enlisted as tribal

Relief carving of a Roman hunting crossbow with its quiver, an ordinary bow and a dagger, 1st–3rd centuries AD. (Musée Crozatier, Le Puy)

Triumphal procession of a Christian Emperor, on the Somerville Gem, Roman 4th century. Note the use of both Imperial and Christian insignia. (University of Pennsylvania Museum, nr. 29-128-3, Philadelphia)

groups. Yet the army remained essentially a mercenary force as the old class of citizens, the basis of ancient Roman armies, had all but disappeared. It was still divided between garrisons and field armies. Local forces consisted of *numerii* of 200 to 400 men under a *tribunus*, one or two being based in each provincial town. Mobile mercenary field forces consisted of light cavalry *foederati* plus heavy cavalry *cataphracti*. The *hippo-toxotai* horse archers formed the fighting elite and proved devastating in North Africa and Italy. Hand picked and highly trained armoured *cataphracti* were not new, but again proved effective, though expensive. On the other hand the Empire now lacked many good horse-raising regions, though Justinian did try to reserve Cappadocia for the breeding of large cavalry mounts.

Central to the new military structure was the *Comitatus* or 'personal army'. Copied by Germanic kings from the Romans in the 3rd century, it was borrowed back by Justinian and his generals Belisarius and Narses. By swearing an oath to those who recruited them rather than to the state, they were naturally seen as a threat to the Emperor; nevertheless such professionals, enlisted on a long-term basis, formed a core around which larger armies could be built. At the heart of the *Comitatus* were the *bucellarii* or personal guards, but even they were prone to mutiny, their success depending almost entirely on the wealth, influence or leadership of their employer.

The Reconquered West

Belisarius was responsible for rebuilding the administration of North Africa. This province, which stretched from Libya to Morocco, was placed under an *Exarch*, an almost autonomous figure with his own military staff and, by the late 6th century, his own army under a *Magister Militum Africae*. The army itself included more cavalry than infantry and consisted of a commander's elite guard, a mobile force of *milites comitatenses* and local *limitanii*. In reconquered Italy the Byzantine authorities faced more serious problems. The barbarian Ostrogoths may have been overthrown but a greater threat now loomed – the Lombards who, in AD 568, poured over the Alps from what is now Austria. Byzantium largely abandoned present-day Lombardy and Tuscany to establish a frontier march in the hills south of Ravenna – still known as *Il Marche*. The *Exarch* of Italy had a field army and a series of garrisons, but the former was too small to halt the Lombards; and so the Empire agreed to share the country, reduced its garrisons and placed them under four regional *Patricians*. The *Patrician* of Sicily was barely involved in mainland affairs, while the others had their

Statuette of a Roman cavalryman, minus his horse, 4th–5th centuries. He wears a lamellar cuirass and thickly padded Iranian-style trousers. *(Met. Museum of Art, J. J. Klejman Gift, 62.7.2, New York)*

fragmented history during the next 1,400 years. The role of Byzantium's *Magister Militum* at Naples merged with that of the local *Dux*, as happened in the Campania south of Rome and perhaps also in Calabria and Apulia. Elsewhere Byzantine control dwindled to isolated coastal cities like Gaeta, Naples and Amalfi. Yet these were the very cities which later took the first steps towards Italy's naval domination of the medieval Mediterranean.

Urban militias, some recruited from new settlers, were vital to defend Italy's city walls where urban life continued – though at a reduced tempo. In Rome a professional mercenary regiment known as the *Theodosiaci* remained after other Byzantine forces were withdrawn in AD 592. Here the Pope was already effectively a ruler, and he even seems to have summoned soldiers from the Balkans. The names of military units elsewhere in Byzantine Italy suggest local and foreign recruitment. The *Veronensium*, for example, may have been Lombards from Verona or Italian refugees from this northern city. Soon local recruits also outnumbered men from the east in the *Exercitus Romanus*, *Exercitus Italiae* and *Exercitus Ravennae*, although such professional forces still remained separate from local militias. Further militia forces were raised by monasteries and land owners within Byzantine territory. Some old Roman imperial families had survived the fall of the Western Empire and still held large estates; now they began to regain long-lost dignities, titles and military roles. While this ancient aristocracy became to some extent Byzantinized, a new elite planted in Italy by Byzantine rulers was gradually Italianized.

After Justinian

Perhaps the most important new formation to emerge under Justinian's successors were the *Optimates* who appeared in the reign of Maurice (AD 582–602). They were probably descended from the *Gothograeci* (Greek Goths) whose own ancestors were Goth prisoners settled in western Anatolia at the end of the 4th century. The *foederati* were now placed under a *Comes Foederatum* based in Thrace, modern Bulgaria, and many *Bucellarii* and other semi-private guard formations were drafted into the regular army. Other regiments included the *Scholae*, who had originally been a crack imperial guard but had now declined to an ornamental palace unit; the *Candidati*,

HQs in Ravenna, Rome and Naples. A smaller fifth force, commanded by a *Dux*, was based at Rimini on the Adriatic coast, while away at the northern end of the Adriatic another *Magister Militum* had a few troops with which to defend Istria and Byzantium's remaining foothold around Venice.

Even so the Lombards broke through in the south, carving out two further duchies at Spoleto and Benevento separated from the Lombard kingdom in northern Italy by a narrow strip of Byzantine territory from Rome to Ravenna. This extraordinary division of the country set the pattern for Italy's who had once been an even more select group of white-uniformed Imperial bodyguards; and the *Domestici*. The *Domestici* of the West had been pensioned off by Theodoric the Goth after he conquered Italy in AD 493, but somehow still existed for Justinian to finally disband half a century later. The *Domestici* of the East also survived as a privileged unit, buying their ranks with cash. The *Excubitores* were a small unit of 300 infantry guards first enrolled by Leo I (AD 457–474) to replace the ineffective *Scholae*; armed with maces, they remained real soldiers for over two centuries but diminished into a parade unit by the early 7th century.

Things were also changing on the frontiers. The steppes of Syria had been abandoned to allied Arab tribes (see below). The frontier *limitanei* of Syria still existed along the edge of the agricultural zone but were gravely under strength. In fact Byzantine Syria was defended in a very localized way, with only few garrisons and some field units in the chief cities. In the war-ravaged Balkans a few demoralized garrisons, plus the cavalry of Thrace, totalled perhaps 15,000 men – the best having been sent to the eastern frontier. By the late 6th century Slav raiders reached the walls of Constantinople itself, and the Emperor's own guards had to chase them away. Until the disastrous Sassanian Iranian occupation of the early 7th century Egypt remained almost untouched by these tumultuous invasions, and here local troops were more like a police force than an army. Until the Sassanians broke through to the Mediterranean the island like Cyprus similarly seemed like a haven of peace, yet as early as AD 578 the Emperor installed military colonists to guard strategic locations. Their importance would, of course, increase when Cyprus was divided between Byzantium and the new power of Islam a century later.

In some ways the organization of 6th century Byzantine armies seems remarkably modern. Units were divided into platoons or *dekarchia* which themselves consisted of small tactical sections led by NCOs. The old centurion had now become an *ekatontarch*, the most senior of whom served as second-in-command to the army's *Comes* rather as the late Roman *Vicarius* had done. An *ilarch* supervised the NCOs and junior officers, and also commanded half a regiment if this was split tactically. Junior officers included the *lochagoi* or *dekarchai*, the

Huge bronze statue of a Christian Emperor, probably Valentian I, last great ruler of the Western Roman Empire (AD 364–375), outside San Sepolcro in Barletta. (Author's photograph)

pentarchai and the *tetrarchai*, all being selected for bravery and intelligence.

The basic military uniform was white, with only guards wearing stylish colours. Even so the *Protectores*, *Domestici*, *Scholae* and *Candidatiti* still had white cloaks. A new form of cape, the *maniakion* of Iranian origin, replaced the Imperial diadem at an Emperor's coronation in the 5th or 6th century, and a version with three buttons was also worn by some *Candidati* guards. Coats with long false sleeves, also of Iranian origin, were seen in Georgia and Armenia in the 7th century and may have indicated the status of *Dux*. Adopted soon after in Byzantium itself, they eventually became the distinctive costume of the Russian aristocracy and of the Ottoman Turks. From the late 6th century belts of Turkish origin with pendant straps were worn as the mark of a soldier and were called 'Bulgarian belts', though they were also criticized for being too elaborate. The Byzantines were, of course, not averse to military splendour, heavy golden neck torques called *campidoctores* being given to loyal retainers when an Emperor was proclaimed. The Byzantine military elite also went against Roman tradition by wearing long hair, though beards were reserved for senior officers.

Recruitment

From Justinian's reign military recruitment was largely voluntary and involved many privileges. Internal recruitment also increased, so that the Empire was less dependent upon barbarians. Supposedly warlike Isauria in southern Anatolia and

Illyria in the Balkans became major sources of recruits. The plains of Thrace provided cavalrymen, despite being ravaged by many invasions, while in Syria a large part of the population seems to have been on the *Dux*'s military payroll.

Nevertheless German soldiers remained important – so much so that their heretical Arian Christian views were tolerated by a society otherwise given to persecuting heretics, Paulicians, Jews and pagans. Goths still provided Byzantium's best heavy cavalry, and in AD 575 more were enlisted into the originally Gothograeci *Optimates*, an elite regiment based in Bithynia throughout the late 6th and 7th centuries. Other Goths settled in military colonies along the Aegean coast. Many were probably Ostrogoths who, escaping the Lombard conquerors of Italy, now fought for Byzantium as spear- and shield-armed cavalry. Other Ostrogoths served as infantry archers. Goth communities survived in the mountains of the Crimea, north of the Black Sea, but seem to have had only a local role. Yet another group of Goths intermarried with Alan nomads from the Russian steppes to form a military aristocracy in the Danube delta.

Various Germanic peoples from north of the Danube were recruited, some 15,000 forming the *Tiberiani* named after Emperor Tiberius I (AD 578–582). Tiberius even recruited Lombards, and a truce in Italy permitted the hard-pressed Byzantines to transfer other Germanic troops to the Balkan front. In addition to Germanic Swabians and Heruli (who gave their name to a form of sword favoured by Byzantine troops) the Empire recruited Sudanese, Arabs, Berbers and Huns.

Tactics

Cavalry were now the dominant arm and still seem to have been divided between spear and archery specialists. Like the Sassanians, Byzantine horse archers shot to order by ranks, but were known for the power of their shots rather than their speed of shooting.

The tactics of the period were described in the earliest Byzantine *tactika* military treatise written by an unknown soldier, perhaps during the reign of

Ivory panel showing the German Stilicho, commander of the Roman West under the Emperor Honorius, c. AD 395 (Cathedral Treasury, Monza)

Romano-Byzantine arms & armour. (A) 4–5 cent helmet from Berkasovo (Vojvod. Mus., Novi Sad); (B) 4–5 cent helmet from Worms (Mus. der Stadt, Worms); (C) 4–5 cent helmet from Intercisa (Nat. Mus., Budapest); (D) 4–5 cent helmet from St. Vid (Waffensammlung, St. Vid no. 3, Vienna); (E) early 5 cent helmet from Concesti (Hermitage, inv. 2160/37, Leningrad); (F) 3–5 cent helmet from Fayum (Coptic Mus., Cairo); (G) 8 cent Turco-Byzantine helmet finial from Gendjik, Kuban area (Hist. Mus., Moscow); (H) mid-late 9 cent Turco-Byzantine helmet from Novorosijsk, Kuban area (Local Mus., Novorosijsk); (I) undated iron visor from Byzantine Great Palace (Arch. Mus., Istanbul); (J) 8 cent Turco-Byzantine iron greaves from Gendjik, Kuban area (Hist. Mus., Moscow); (K) 10 cent gilded bronze shield boss from Ain Dara (Arch. Mus., nr. 1/64, Aleppo); (L) part of 6–7 cent shield boss from Nocera Umbra (Mus. Alto Medioevo, Rome); (M) 4 cent crossbow bolt head with shaft shown by dotted line, from Halterm (Schweizerischen Waffen Inst., Zurich); (N) 4 cent sword from Cologne (location unknown); (O) 6–early 7 cent sword from Aphrodisias, perhaps Sassanian, length 1.8 metres (site museum, Aphrodisias); (P) 4 cent axe from Istanbul (Dumbarton Oaks Coll., Washington); (Q) 6–8 cent axe from Butrint, northern Albania (ex-Anamali); (R) ceremonial spearhead supposedly used by Justinian, with later decoration (location unknown); (S) 6 cent Turco-Byzantine spearhead from Corinth (location unknown).

Justinian. Most of this work deals with fortification, suggesting that the author was an engineer. It also referred to enemies capturing Byzantine outposts by 'wearing our equipment', and of the use of fires and smoke for signalling. In discussing open battle tactics the writer relied on ancient texts and archaic terms, though he did contrast these with his own day, e.g. when he stated that troops were drawn up in squares or oblongs instead of the old phalanx. The four front ranks and those at the sides would be armed with long spears, those behind having javelins. Armour, he insisted, should be worn over a thickly padded garment, as should helmets. Cavalry formations were the same as the infantry, though in looser order. In camp men slept in tents with spears stuck in the ground at their feet, shields leaning against these spears and other equipment on their left side. When putting on equipment men should start at their feet, then legs, thighs, body, helmets, sword belt, archery equipment and last of all shoulder pieces. In battle, our anonymous writer suggested, the elite should be in the centre of the first and second lines, with the Bucellarii guards held back as a reserve around the commander.

Among many interesting details were instructions on how infantry archers should defend themselves against cavalry attack. Their first two ranks shot at the presumably unarmoured legs of the enemy's horses, while men further back shot high to drop arrows on a foe who, the writer stated, could not raise his shield while riding. Cavalry would not yet have had stirrups. As the enemy closed, the infantry picked up spears which until then had lain on the ground. At night, he suggested, men carrying lanterns should be fully armoured. Ambushes, he wrote almost regretfully, were now a common tactic even among 'Romans' (Byzantines); and when making a feigned retreat non-essential equipment like sword scabbards could be dropped to add authenticity.

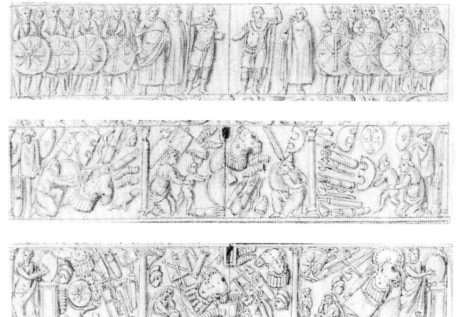

Carved reliefs on the lost Column of Arcadius in Constantinople, c. AD 400, in an 18th century drawing. The soldiers are unarmoured, except for large round shields, while the two Emperors wear antique 'muscle cuirasses'. The lower panels show Roman and enemy equipment including antique 'muscle cuirasses', helmets with complete facial visors, quilted or laminated arm and leg protections, plus assorted weapons. (Trinity Coll. Library, Cambridge)

Where archery was concerned, a thumb draw was the strongest though other methods should also be used to avoid tiring the hand. Rapidity of shooting was, he declared, a matter of practice not technique, and it was also a good idea to shoot at an angle to the enemy's ranks so as to get around their shields.

On the field of battle Byzantine commanders did use sophisticated tactics. At Taginae in AD 552, Narses placed dismounted *foederati* across the Flavian Way with infantry archers thrown forward on either side. Behind the archers and protecting them were Narses' elite cavalry, with a further force of archers and cavalry on high ground to the left ready for a counterattack. The Ostrogoth enemy charged the Byzantine centre several times but were repulsed. Narses advanced, the Ostrogoths broke and the battle was won. Two years later at Capua the Byzantines again used a mixed force of infantry and horse archers to achieve victory. Analysis of such battles also suggests that spear-armed Byzantine infantry fought in close order behind their shields whereas infantry archers operated in looser formation.

Byzantine heavy cavalry remained a once-only shock weapon, but during the 6th century large, densely packed formations of Byzantine and Sassanian horsemen both failed against steppe nomads. As a result both armies divided their cavalry into smaller units with defensive, offensive and reserve sections. On the other hand the Byzantines did have some advantages against nomadic peoples such as the Avars, particularly when fighting in the Balkans. In winter the nomads' horses were in poor condition, while at night nomads were vulnerable because they did not generally make strongly fortified encampments. During campaigns against such mobile enemies Byzantine troops carried many days' food, and in winter operated from headquarters at Odessus (mod. Varna) or on the Thracian plain.

Against the Sassanians in the East the Byzantines evolved a strategy of guerrilla warfare, tactics which lay behind the famous 'Shadowing Warfare' later used against Muslim Arabs. In this wild and mountainous terrain horses, mules and camels provided beasts of burden. After the defeat of a Sassanian army in AD 575 at Malatya 24 elephants were also captured, but they were sent to Constantinople as booty. Almost more important than tactics was the question of morale, and Byzantine leaders paid close attention to this. Byzantium's role as the Christian Empire was central to its morale. Careful religious preparations preceded a battle, relics being paraded before the troops including images 'not made by human hand', which had a profound impact upon the men's minds.

TRIUMPH AND DISASTER

The 7th and 8th centuries have been described as Byzantium's Dark Age. In Europe large parts of what are now Yugoslavia, Bulgaria and northern Greece were lost to Slav and Bulgar invaders, while Byzantine control in Italy grew feeble. The Sassanians finally broke through the ancient frontier between the Romano-Byzantine and Iranian empires, conquering eastern Anatolia, Syria, Palestine and Egypt. The Byzantines did drive the Sassanians out a generation later, but then North Africa, Egypt, Syria, Cyprus and eastern Anatolia were again lost, this time to the Muslim Arabs.

Before the reign of Heraclius (AD 610–641) the army consisted of spear-armed infantry with a small but tactically dominant cavalry force. Maurice (AD 582–602) tried to set up a territorial reserve of infantry archers, training once a week, but whether this got off the ground is unclear. The Byzantine army then collapsed in the civil war and Sassanian invasion which followed Maurice's death. During the struggle between Phocas (AD 602–610) and Heraclius, anti-Phocas forces in Alexandria included regular soldiers, barbarian mercenaries, sailors, urban volunteers and the Green Circus Faction. These Circus Factions were more than supporters' clubs, acting like political gangs in the Empire's main cities. Supporters of Phocas in Constantinople included militias based upon other Circus Factions, plus sailors of the Egyptian fleet who, however, soon deserted to Heraclius.

When he at last gained power Heraclius rebuilt an army out of this wreckage. He gathered scattered, leaderless but numerous troops, equipping the elite regiments and restructuring others. While working on existing foundations, Heraclius took his Avar foes as an ideal. His main problem remained a lack of horse archers, the cutting edge of a new army which took two years to reorganize and train. Heraclius then broke tradition by leading this army into battle; moreover, he personally slew the Sassanian general Razates in single combat – here the Emperor was wounded in the mouth while his horse was injured in the flank, despite its lamellar armour. It has been suggested that Heraclius's military reforms were also influenced by his childhood in North Africa, where the provincial Byzantine army was characterized by larger military units.

Although North Africa remained untouched even during the Sassanian occupation of Egypt, the rise of the Muslim Arabs led to a withdrawal of Byzantine forces to the coast after AD 647. By AD 697 all that remained in Byzantine hands was the isolated port of Ceuta on the southern side of the Straits of Gibraltar. Byzantium had already lost its possessions in Spain, except for the Balearic Islands.

Byzantine rule in Egypt was very unpopular among a Coptic majority, who were in turn regarded as heretics by the Orthodox Greeks. Militarily Byzantine Egypt incorporated Barqa and Tripolitania in what is now Libya, and was defended by five *Duces*, that of Alexandria being the senior. Each had a small army consisting of local levies stiffened by the *bucellarii* and intended to deter nomad raiders. The *Dux* of Alexandria had an elite guard of black Africans but the most experienced *Dux* appears to

Soldiers at 'Trojan Council' in the early 5th century Virgilius Vaticanus *manuscript. They wear short-sleeved mail hauberks with mail coifs as seen on 3rd century wall paintings from Dura Europos in Syria. (Vatican Lib., Ms. Lat. 3225 f. 73v, Rome)*

have been the governor of Thebais in the south. His well-trained fórce included horse archers and spear-armed cavalry to face the warlike Nubians. In the event the *Thebaid Dux* did not contribute to the defence of Egypt until the Muslims reached his own province, while forces in Barqa and Tripolitania took no part at all. In Syria Antioch's Circus Factions put up a spirited resistance to the Sassanians, but when the Arabs arrived a generation later they seem to have gone over to the rising power of Islam. In fact the Muslim Arabs defeated the fragmented Byzantine defenders of Syria one by one – just as in Egypt.

Theme & Tagmata system

Following the staggering conquests by the Muslim Arabs in the 7th century there were fundamental changes to Byzantine military organization. The most important was the establishment of *theme* or regional armies and of *tagmata* or central armies based around the capital. Maurice may already have settled military colonies in the East in the late 6th century, and it is also unclear whether real *themes* emerged under Heraclius or only after the Muslims started raiding deep into Anatolia. That a soldier's family should inherit his military obligations was well established, while the difficulty of paying units dispersed during the chaos of the Muslim attacks further encouraged soldiers to settle down, gain property and even part-time jobs. The first *theme* that clearly emerged as a territorial unit was the *Opsikion*, followed some years later by the *Anatolikon* and the *Armeniakon*. *Opsikion* forces served as an Imperial reserve until the late 7th century – though not always successfully – but were downgraded to an ordinary *theme* army following an early 8th century rebellion. After this the troops of the *Anatolikon* and *Armeniakon themes* proved more effective than those of the *Opsikion*. Continuing Muslim raids also led to the Byzantine frontier being further subdivided into

small *kleisourai* zones but these would not develop into the multitude of *themes* typical of later Byzantium until after a civil war in AD 742–3.

An increasing sense of *theme* pride and identity characterized the late 7th and 8th centuries, though such rivalries could lead *theme* armies to take opposite sides in Byzantium's many civil wars. Meanwhile the government permitted troops to acquire land with which to support themselves; but this did not mean that the soldiers turned into farmers – rather, they lived off the produce of their land as did medieval knights. The nucleus of *theme* forces remained properly equipped regulars, as in the *tagmata* armies. Some lived on their estates, others lived in barracks. The equipment of poorer troops seems to have been

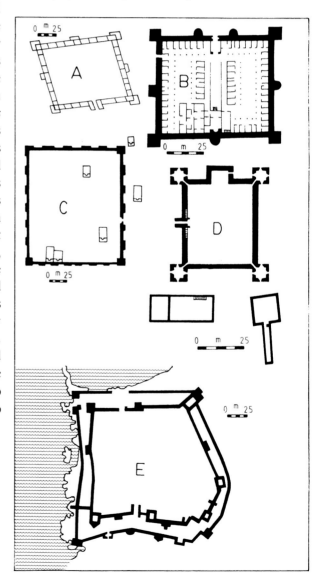

(A) Asymmetrical late Roman fortress at Seba Mgata, North Africa (after Fentress); (B) late Roman fort at Castra Dionysias, Egypt (after Carrie); (C) 4–8 cent fortified town with churches inside & outside walls, Umm al Rasas, Jordan (after Kennedy & Riley); (D) late 3–early 4 cent fort with two external water cisterns, Khan Aneybeh, Syria (after Kennedy & Riley); (E) 5–6 cent, 9 cent & 12–13 cent fortifications of Corycus, including two typical 9 cent Byzantine 'keel' towers, Turkey (after Foss & Winfield).

purchased by their fellow villagers, by the state, or by richer landowners. An elite fought as cavalry and formed the minor aristocracy of a region, while much of the remainder fought on foot.

While it was possible for a man to rise from a *theme* army – Leo III (AD 717–741) even became Emperor – the elite guards units were the source of most senior officers. By the late 8th century the old *Domestici* had been assimilated into the *Scholae* who, having been reformed by Constantine V (AD 741–775), again had a proper military role. The *Spatharii*, founded by Theodosius II back in the 5th century, originally consisted of sword-bearing eunuchs; from the 7th century, however, they included promising young officers who, in addition to being physically complete, were trained for higher rank. The Empress Irene (AD 797–802) created her own bodyguard known as the *Vigla* originally withdrawn from one of the *themes* – probably the *Thrakasion* from Thrace – but after her death it also declined in status.

Below these elite formations were *Tagmata* troops based around the capital. Each *tagma* consisted of 300 men as a tactical unit. Ten *tagma* formed a *meros* regiment, and between the two stood the *moera*, of which two or three normally formed a *meros*. In theory an army consisted of three *meros*. Early in the 9th century Nicephoros I (AD 802–811) divided the *Tagmata* into Imperial and provincial *Tagmata*, the former still being based around Constantinople. He also set up the *Hikanatoi*, possibly as a training unit for cadets. *Tagmata* soldiers were now protected by law against the severest of punishments even if found guilty, and had better pay and equipment than other troops. Nevertheless Byzantine soldiers remained prone to revolt. The worst centre of disturbance was Thrace, the *theme* closest to the capital, and even elite corps rioted over lack of pay in the 7th century. Unrest was also caused by bad leadership, defeat, loss of territory, or even government policy in general.

Meanwhile the Muslim-Byzantine frontier had stabilized along the Taurus mountains and north towards Georgia. The only major change came with the Umayyad Caliphate's conquest of Cilicia and Malatya in the late 7th and early 8th centuries, while Cappadocia (between modern Konya and Kayseri) became the headquarters and mustering point for Byzantine resistance. As the years passed there was a blurring of identities across this war-torn frontier,

'Battle between Trojans and Greeks' in the late 5th century Virgilius Romanus manuscript, which already has much in common with medieval art. The large round shields, scale, lamellar or highly stylized mail shirts, broad-bladed spears and simplified archery equipment also seem halfway between late Roman and early medieval styles. (Vat. Library, Ms. Lat. 3867, Rome)

and soldiers changed religion with remarkable ease – usually from Christianity to Islam.

Byzantine control was also tenuous in many Western provinces; in what is now Albania, for example, most forces were based on family or tribal loyalties. In AD 697–8 the people of Italy's Venetian lagoon set up their own duchy, though the election of its *Doge* still had to be ratified by Constantinople. In AD 726 the Byzantine citizens of Ravenna successfully resisted an increase in Imperial control when their own *iuvenes* defeated a Byzantine expeditionary force. The population of Ravenna had, in fact, already been divided into twelve sections, eleven of them providing armed *bandi* to help the *numeri* of the garrison while the twelfth was reserved for the clergy. Elsewhere Byzantine Italy suffered periodic Lombard raiding, the most effective defence being organized by the Pope in Rome rather than the Imperial government in Constantinople. Rome's small army, organized along the same lines as other Byzantine forces, was a major power in Italian affairs. In the late 8th century most of its troops were part-time militia but there was a small elite *Scholae Militiae*. Units were led by *patroni* from the local Roman aristocracy

'Abraham and Melkizadek', on a mosaic of AD 432–440. Though stylized, these mosaics contain interesting details such as the decorated neck opening of the leading soldier's mail hauberk. (In situ, Basilica of Santa Maria Maggiore, Rome)

and marched behind their own *bandon* flags. In AD 800, however, the Pope crowned Charlemagne as Emperor and the city of Rome, with its surrounding territory, ceased to form part of the Romano-Byzantine Empire for ever.

Recruitment

Changes in the Empire's borders inevitably led to changes in the recruitment of the Byzantine army. At the start of the 7th century most of the Empire's light cavalry came from barbarian peoples. Maurice had, however, enlisted Isaurians and Cappadocians from within Imperial Anatolia, Illyrians from the Byzantine Balkans, Armenians, captured Sassanians, Huns, Bulgars and Lombards from beyond the frontiers. The captured Sassanians were sent to the West, Bulgars to various areas including North Africa. The core of Heraclius' army, however, were Greek-speakers from the Pontus and Isaurian regions of Anatolia, though allied Armenians and Georgians from the Caucasus were also present. Almost all officers were Greek.

One group who played a significant role in early clashes with the Muslims were the *Mardaites* (Arabic: *Jarajima*) of the Syrian coastal mountains. Whether the Emperor stirred up their guerrilla resistance is unknown, but the Byzantines certainly took advantage of their actions. These *Mardaites* have been identified as being descended from Byzantine *limitanii*, but are more likely to have been superficially Christian mountainfolk who resisted any authority – including the previous Byzantine rulers. After being defeated by the Muslim Arabs in AD 708 some came to terms with their new rulers, though others migrated to Byzantine territory to settle as warrior communities in southern Anatolia, Greece and some Greek islands. Around the same time Justinian II also tried to transfer part of the Cypriot population closer to the capital to serve in the Imperial navy.

By the 8th century the Byzantine army contained far fewer foreigners. Recruitment to the privileged *Tagmata* regiments was still carefully controlled, entrants being aged 18 to 40 and excluding slaves, exiles, clergy or previously disgraced soldiers. Men of *Gothograeci* origin continued to play a role in the *Optimates* based in Bithynia, but this was not the elite it once had been, largely declining to garrison status by the 8th century. Religious tension between Greeks and Armenians increased and, perhaps as a result, efforts were made to recruit Slavs. Justinian II forcibly transferred 30,000 from the Balkans to the *Opsikion theme*, but after a brief clash many defected to Islam. In the 9th century units were mixed and their recruitment varied in an effort to reduce religious and ethnic clashes. Anatolian soldiers were transferred to the Balkans, recruitment from hill peoples within the Empire was further increased, and barbarian *foederati* were settled as provincial *Tagmata*. Turks had already been welcomed around Sinop on the Black Sea, while Iranian Muslim deserters were warmly welcomed. So short of military manpower had Byzantium become that Theophilus (AD 829–842) begged for Venetian and

Frankish volunteers, though whether any came remains unknown. Foreign *Hetaireia* formed a new guard for Michael II (AD 820–829), while black troops of probable Muslim origin became Theophilus' favourite guards unit.

Cities had militias, but that of Constantinople was the most important and seems to have been partly based upon Circus Factions. The Blue Faction contributed to the Walls regiment, the Green Faction to the *Noumera* regiment, both of which had existed since the 6th century. At first their training was minimal, but it seems to have improved after the Muslim siege of AD 674–8. Other militias were based on craft guilds.

Tactics

The so-called *Strategikon of Emperor Maurice*, which was probably written early in the reign of Heraclius, shows deep concern for discipline, morale and control; in fact Byzantine *tactica* treatises seem preoccupied with treachery in the officer corps, noting that rebels often won support by promising more pay and promotion. Heraclius trained his troops in mock battles and manoeuvres before marching on the Sassanians. Even then he first sent light cavalry against Arab tribes, encouraging them to revert to their old Byzantine allegiance. The subsequent campaign against the Sassanians was hard but successful, but more than once the enemy failed to fall for a feigned retreat.

Shortage of manpower forced the Byzantine command to move troops over huge distances, and in AD 687–8, for example, a cavalry force was hurriedly transferred from Anatolia to the Balkans to crush a Slav invasion. The normal way of countering Slav light infantry tactics was to use Byzantine light infantry archers and javelin men, backed up by armoured infantry. Troops also had to be highly trained. Cavalry exercise grounds, comparable to those of the Roman Empire and later Muslim armies, still existed. Byzantine troops may also have continued the Roman *Causa Exercitii* military tattoos in the capital. Training probably reflected the ideal

tactics described in the *Strategikon*, with spear-armed cavalry in the centre and horse archers on the flanks. Nevertheless the evidence of battle suggests that Byzantine discipline was inferior to that of the Sassanians and Muslim Arabs. Among other differences, Byzantine cavalry mounts were hobbled and left to graze – a habit typical of armies used to relatively rich grasslands – while Sassanian horses were fed on gathered forage, typical of armies from a semi-desert land. Byzantine forces also tended to stick to the mountains, their Sassanian foes preferring the plains. Byzantine horsemen were trained to fight on foot and Byzantine infantry used sudden attacks to force Sassanian cavalry into close combat, attacking the unarmoured bellies of Sassanian horses.

During the long centuries of conflict with Islam Byzantine horse archery declined, to be replaced by the lancers who became the most important section of the army. They were, however, rarely able to face infantry archers unless the latter broke formation. The standard Byzantine tactic of the 7th and 8th centuries seems to have placed armoured horse behind the infantry, with light cavalry covering their flanks. Heavy cavalry would then charge through

'Israelites attack Hai', on the same early 5th century mosaics. Already the soldiers' equipment has more in common with that of early Byzantine rather than late Roman armies. (In situ, Basilica of Santa Maria Maggiore, Rome)

openings made by the infantry. Until Turks came to dominate Muslim forces in the 10th century this was also the case on the other side of the frontier. Not until the 9th century was there a small revival of Byzantine horse archery, but then such troops were mostly Turkish mercenaries who used harassment tactics.

Large-scale confrontations were now rare and often disastrous. In AD 708 a Byzantine army stood against an Arab raid at the northern end of the Cilician Gates, the main pass through the Taurus Mountains, only to suffer a crushing defeat. Generally the *theme* system meant that troops were scattered, and concentrating them against a Muslim raid proved difficult. Consequently, the sophisticated strategy of 'Shadowing Warfare' was developed. Being unable to stop the raids, Byzantium attempted to limit damage and regain spoils as the enemy made his way home through the mountains. For their part Muslim armies rarely took towns, instead demanding ransom in return for leaving their surroundings intact. Not that raiding was easy: the towering Taurus Mountains formed, in the words of the Arab geographer Ibn Hawqal, 'a barrier between the two worlds of Islam and Christendom'. In such terrain the Byzantines even made barriers of burning tree trunks though early 9th century Muslim *nafatin* 'incendiary troops' could extinguish such a barricade through their use of special fireproof clothing.

Meanwhile relations between the two sides could be very civilized. The Caliph Harun al Rashid returned some prisoners, including one described as a 'princess', as a gesture to the Emperor Nicephoros I, after Harun marched right across Anatolia to seize Heraclea (mod. Eregli) on the Black Sea coast. There had long been special arrangements to exchange POWs at specified frontier points, and even as early as the mid-7th century there are records of captives and captors becoming personal friends.

In such warfare communications were vital. Byzantine flags were used for signalling and as rallying points, a dark *kamelafkion* banner indicating the start of a battle. Others showed where each unit was to set up its tents in camp. The *Strategikon of Maurice* stated that although a *flammula* lance pennon looked handsome it got in the way, and should be removed when one mile from the enemy. Some *flammula* were double or swallow-tailed, which may betray Avar influence, though triple-tailed types did not come in until the 11th century. The most important banners were very ancient, being kept in a special store and constantly repaired, while silver crosses on top of flag poles came into use late in the 9th century. The most common motif appears to have been a cross, the most popular colours being dark blue (perhaps actually black or purple), lighter blue, red, white, green and yellow. In theory the shape and colour of a banner indicated the identity and size of a unit. Ideally every section in a *meros* used the same colour, each small *moira* adding different coloured streamers. The baggage train also counted as a *moira* with its own flag. If a flag was captured its colour guard would be reduced to the ranks, though this did not stop the Byzantine losing many banners: about 300 *bandas* were found in the Sassanian capital, among the enemy's own flags, when this fell to the Byzantines.

Warriors in the late 5th century Ilias Ambrosiana *manuscript appear in much more archaic equipment than those in the* Virgilius Vaticanus *or* Virgilius Romanus. *On the other hand they have similarities with lightly armoured troops in early Byzantine manuscripts. (Bib. Ambrosiana, Cod. F.205 Inf, Milan)*

REVIVAL AND COUNTERATTACK

Before the Byzantine Empire could counterattack its many foes the government had to regain real control over territories which still recognized its rule. Many areas – like Kherson in the Crimea, the Dalmatian coast, Venice, Amalfi and Gaeta in Italy – were effectively autonomous. Even in Greece coastal refuges and off-shore islands were virtually free before Imperial control was reimposed in AD 804–6. During the early 9th century the Emperor regained control of the Albanian coast and sent military colonists to Cyprus, which was a neutral condominium shared with the Muslims until reconquered by Byzantium in AD 964–5. Byzantine interests in Cyprus were the responsibility of the *Kibyrraeotic theme* in southern Anatolia, which also had the task of attacking Muslim Cilicia by sea while *theme* armies of the interior attacked it by land. Each Byzantine advance was followed by military colonization and the establishment of monasteries, though these sometimes played into enemy hands. The Empire's brutal suppression of the Paulician 'heretics' of the Eastern frontier pushed them into the arms of the Emir of Malatya, whose strongly walled city was the centre of Muslim resistance. An eastward offensive by Michael III (AD 842–867) failed and resulted in a counterattack by the Emir of Malatya. This, however, was itself disastrously defeated – opening up the east to Byzantine invasion early in the 10th century (see MAA 89 – *Byzantine Armies 886–1118*).

Roman soldier on a carved ivory plaque showing the 'Life of St. Paul', 5th century Italy. Note the short sword suspended from a scabbard slide, and the wide trousers. (Bargello Mus., Florence)

Organization

The armies which carried out Byzantium's 9th century revival were basically the same as those of a century earlier, though more is known about them. An army division or *turma* consisted of from three to five *drungaroi* which in turn consisted of five *banda*, each *banda* having 200 to 400 men. A *turmach* commanded a *turma*, of whom there were normally three in each *theme*. He was junior to a general and often had the rank of *protospatharios*.

The Byzantine attitude towards its soldiers was generally very tolerant, recognizing their need for dignity. The military ideal was summed up by the *akritoi* border warriors, whose exploits are celebrated in the epic poem *Digenes Akritas*. As defenders of far-flung frontiers these *akritoi* had much in common with the semi-independent Margraves of medieval Germany or the Cossacks of Russia. Meanwhile in the *theme* armies there was a drift back to the old system of paying troops in cash. The elite *tagmata* lived solely on cash payments; but until Byzantine military dominance was assured the pay caravans made tempting targets both for the enemy and bandits.

Back in Constantinople the ceremonial role of units whose military value was now minimal may

'Guards of Theodosius I' on a silver plate made in AD 388. Note the heavy torques around the soldiers' necks, given as a mark of rank and loyalty. (Real Acad. de la Historia, Madrid)

▶ Shield decorations. The first nine & a half lines (listed left to right) are taken from a copy of the 4th–5th century Notitia Dignitatum manuscript. It was copied a thousand years after the original, so the unit insignia have been simplified and in some cases misunderstood, although some do appear in Late Roman or early Byzantine art. (1st line) Matiary Seniores; Daci; Scythae; Sabarienses; Ocianani; Thebei; Cimbriani; (2nd line) Primani; Undecimani; Lanceary iunior; Regii; Armigeri Junio; Cornuti; Brachiati; Petulantes; (3rd line) Cornuti; Britones Seniores; Ascarii Seniores; Celtae Senio; Heruli Senio; Batani; Mattiaci; (4th line) Ascarii Juniores; Tubantes; Constantimani; Mattiaci iunior; Ascarii Senio; Ascarii Junio; Joumi Senior; Faelic. Arcad. Junio; (5th line) Sagittarii Sen. Orientales; Sagittarii Junior. Orient.; Sagittary Dnei; (6th line) Unidices; Bucinobantes; Falchouarii; Thraces; (7th line) Terumigi; Faelices Thedodosian; Faelices Arcadiani; (8th line) Scoti Theodosiani; IV Theodosiani; Armigeri Senior; Morsicianci; (9th line) Joumiani; Herculiani; Dinitenses; (10th line) Tongraecani; Pannoniciani; (the following shield patterns are taken from Late Roman or Byzantine art) silver dish of Valentian I, late 4 cent (Mus. d'Art, Geneva) & Coptic wood carving, 5–6 cents (Berlin); drawing of the lost Column of Arcadius in Constantinople (Trin. Coll., Cambridge); (11th line) drawing of the lost Column of Arcadius in Constantinople (Trin. Coll., Cambridge); fragments of lost Column of Theodosius I (Bayazit Hamam, Istanbul), 'Triumph of Constantius II' on 4 cent silver dish (Hermitage, Leningrad) & 'Guards of Justinian' on 6 cent mosaic (Church of San Vitale, Ravenna); 'Old Testament scenes' on early 5 cent mosaic (Basilica of Santa Maria Maggiore, Rome); 'Old Testament scenes' on early 5 cent mosaic (Basilica of Santa Maria Maggiore, Rome); (12th line) carved ivory panel showing General Stilicho, c. AD 395 (Cath. Treasury, Monza); 'Guards of Theodosius I' on silver plate of AD 388 (Acad. de la Historia, Madrid); carved ivory box from 6 cent Egypt (Brit. Mus., London), drawing of the lost Column of Arcadius in Constantinople (Trin. Coll., Cambridge) & Coptic wood carving, 5–6 cents (Berlin); hunting scene on mosaic of AD 315–350 (Piazza Armerina, Sicily); hunting scene on mosaic of AD 315–350 (Piazza Armerina, Sicily); carved shield on Arch of Constantine, early 4 cent (Rome); Homilies of Gregory of Nazianzus, 9 cent (Bib. Nat., Paris).

have led to the retention of archaic uniforms. The 'shoulder tufts' mentioned in the *Tactica* of Emperor Leo VI (AD 886–912) are an example, perhaps being comparable to the *pteruges* shoulder fringes of an earlier age. Though elite units and their commanders wore specified colours on ceremonial occasions, there is little evidence that the 9th century Byzantine army was uniformed in a modern sense. Byzantine heraldry is also something of a mystery. The double-headed imperial eagle was perhaps known in 10th century Anatolia – though on the Muslim side of the frontier – and was not used by Byzantine Emperors until the time of Alexius Comnenus (AD 1081–1118). Griffins

were the 'heraldic' animals most often mentioned in *Digenes Akritas*. Elsewhere there is a reference to a soldier with St. John painted on his shield, another somewhat later with a gold horseman on his shield, and to a Byzantine leader in Sicily who identified himself by a wild plant in his helmet.

Recruitment

In some regions many men had military obligations and could be summoned for inspection, though only the best equipped were used. A *theme* soldier too poor

to equip himself properly might become a military servant, an irregular (literally known as a 'cattle thief'), or could enter the *dzekones* garrison troops. By the 10th century, and perhaps earlier, the eastern *theme* soldier was almost identical to his Muslim counterpart. But of course Muslim frontier troops were now also of mixed origins, Iranian cavalry, converted Slav deserters and Syrian Arabs having settled in Antioch, Cilicia and the Taurus Mountains from the 7th to 10th centuries.

On the Byzantine side Iranian defectors settled on the Black Sea coast, retaining a separate identity into the 9th century. Turks from the Ferghana valley in Central Asia were similarly incorporated into the Byzantine army as skilled horse archers, and Khazars from the vast Jewish Turkish khanate north of the Black Sea served as allies and mercenaries.

Byzantine relations with Muslim Arab POWs were quite cordial, the Empire hoping that these skilled warriors would convert and so add to the Empire's military potential. A special ceremony seems to have accompanied the arrival of such prisoners in Constantinople. At a signal they would lie on their faces while guards held their spears reversed; at a second signal they would stand again while the guards turned their spears upright. In the capital Arab prisoners watched the Hippodrome races and attended banquets dressed in white tunics without belts. They had a mosque, and on at least one occasion helped defend the city walls against the Bulgars.

Tactics

The guerrilla concepts of 'Shadowing Warfare' remained central to Byzantine strategy well into the 10th century but, as the Empire adopted an increasingly aggressive policy towards its Muslim neighbours, a higher proportion of eastern *theme* armies consisted of cavalry. In various respects the Byzantines copied their Arab foes, or 'adopted from the Ishmaelites' as they put it. Intelligence about enemy plans was eagerly sought, spies posing as merchants entering enemy territory before the raiding season began. Soldiers dressed as farmers would be left along the raiders' expected route, while other men, wearing dull-coloured *epanoklibania* surcoats as a form of camouflage, watched the enemy as he penetrated Byzantine territory. A small cavalry rearguard known as a *saka* (from the Arabic *saqah*) might retreat ahead of the foe, who himself sent out cavalry sections several days ahead of his main body of troops. The task of these advance units was to survey the land and select quarters for the invaders. Byzantine troops would in turn try to cut off these advance sections.

When ambushing an enemy men should be placed on both sides of the road supported by cavalry some

▲ *'Guards of the Emperor Justinian' on a mid-6th century mosaic. Note the Christian monogram on the shield, and the large jewelled torques around the necks of these troops. (In situ church of San Vitale, Ravenna)*

▼ *Panel showing 'Defeat of Ai by the Israelites' on a Byzantine carved ivory box, 8th–10th centuries. Only the defeated wear turbans, which suggests the artist identified the troops of Ai with the Muslims, the Hebrews with Byzantines. The latter have archaic cuirasses or loose tunics with one arm bared, round shields with a large horizontal grip, and long broad but non-tapering swords. (Victoria & Albert Museum, inv. 247–1865, London)*

way off. It was generally easier to hit the enemy as he made his way home, and leaders were advised only to use heavy cavalry as skirmishers if an enemy were few in number. Ideally a Byzantine commander would occupy broken terrain ahead of the enemy, infantry holding the heights while cavalry took position in open areas. Water sources had to be controlled, particularly in the passes. Here infantry could block narrow gorges, shield men standing in front with archers and javelin throwers behind them and on either side. On the other hand, Muslim raiders often left ambushes to catch those who were shadowing them. They also kept back selected infantry to form a shield wall behind which the foragers could retreat if attacked by the Byzantines.

Leo VI's *Tactika* advised Byzantine archers to use poisoned arrows against the Muslims' horses, a tactic which may have been adopted from the Slavs. By the 10th century the Byzantine bow was almost one and a half metres long, with arrows about 0.7 metres long. The arrow-guide or *solenarion*, first mentioned in the 6th century, had also become a common light infantry weapon. Even more terrifying was Greek Fire: flame-throwing syphons which could 'cover ten men' were one of the main Byzantine military developments, and these were sometimes used even in open battle as well as in siege warfare.

ALLIES AND NEIGHBOURS

The following section deals with Serbs, Bulgarians, Georgians, Armenians, Kurds, Arab Ghassanids and Berbers. The peoples of the Russian steppes and those of the earlier Middle East have been covered by Elite 30, *Attila and the Nomad Hordes* and MAA 243, *Rome's Enemies (5): The Desert Frontier*, while the Germanic peoples of early Medieval Europe will be the subject of a forthcoming Men-at-Arms title.

Allied forces played an important role in late Roman and Byzantine military thinking, yet their unreliability was recognized. The *Strategikon of Maurice* specifically warned commanders to keep

allies in the dark about their plans as they might desert to the enemy. Various peoples, or *ethnika*, also differed in their techniques, amenability to discipline, and general level of civilization, such characteristics being highlighted in military treatises.

Serbs

Most numerous of the peoples who invaded Byzantium's Balkan provinces were the Slavs, and of these the Serbs were the most threatening. Yet the largely infantry Serb clans, under their competing *zupan* chiefs, only posed a major problem when led by nomad conquerors like the Bulgars or Avars. They were also vulnerable in winter, when the bare trees offered little cover and their tracks might be visible in the snow. Though poor in weapons, the Slavs were numerous and tough, mostly using small javelins and large rectangular shields. They preferred to ambush their enemies in woods and mountains but, if forced to fight in the open, would make a single wild infantry charge. Despite poisoned arrows, archery was of minor importance to southern Slav warriors who, in addition to javelins, used spears, knives and, from the late 8th century, war axes. Swords, like the little armour they possessed, were reserved for a ruling elite.

Bulgarians

(See Elite 30, *Attila and the Nomad Hordes* for the earlier history of the Bulgars.)

The Bulgars were originally a Turkish people within the military traditions of the Central Asian steppes. Their first recorded state in southern Russia collapsed in the mid-7th century, after which some fled into the Balkans, where they established the nation still known as Bulgaria. The Turkish ruling elite of this new kingdom was, however, soon absorbed by its largely Slav subjects, leaving little more than its name. The Bulgars had, in fact, ceased to be strictly nomadic before crossing the Danube in AD 679, and they soon adopted many Byzantine military techniques.

Bulgaria was rich, and the Bulgars had a sophisticated Hunnish military tradition on which to build, yet Byzantine ideas would dominate after Bulgaria converted to Christianity in AD 864. An aristocracy of *boyars* continued to provide leadership and to advise the Khan, while a *Tarkhan* served as the ruler's chief military officer. Turkish Bulgars formed a cavalry elite, but the bulk of the army consisted of Slav infantry. The Khan also had a personal retinue which, regarded in Byzantium as a bodyguard, probably consisted of personal companions in the Turco-Mongol tradition. The early Bulgarian army was more effective in raids or ambushes than open battle, and was still rewarded by booty instead of pay; but by the time of Khan Krum in the early 9th century it had become more regular, and had even earned a reputation in siege warfare. Bulgaria's conversion to Christianity also led to Turkish horse-tail banners being replaced by Christian flags. A new Christian code of military behaviour stipulated when wars might be fought, but did not inhibit the great Khan Symeon from slitting the noses of all his Byzantine captives. The 9th century Bulgar army now attacked in ordered ranks, 'unlike all other Scythian nations' according to the Emperor Leo VI, and a small corps of military engineers appeared. Arms, armour and arsenals were regularly inspected,

and a small though particularly well-equipped elite was kept in permanent readiness.

Bulgars had earlier been settled as *foederati* in Thrace and eastern Macedonia by the Byzantine Emperor Justinian II as a bastion against Avar invasion, and Bulgarian POWs continued to be enlisted by the Byzantines during the 8th and 9th centuries. One would have expected Bulgarian fortifications in the Balkans – an area which formed one of the richest provinces of the Roman and Byzantine Empires – to reflect only Western building techniques; but the structures erected at Pliska, the first Balkan Bulgarian capital, include influences from far away in Central Asia. How these reached the banks of the Danube through the vicissitudes of Bulgar history remains a mystery.

Georgians

Medieval Georgia consisted of Lazica on the Black Sea coast and Iberia inland to the east. A third northern region of Abkhazia, where the Caucasus Mountains came down to the Black Sea, could be added. Iberia was the heartland of the medieval Georgia and officially converted to Christianity in AD 330, though pagans existed for another two centuries. Meanwhile the ruling dynasty of Iberia, though of Iranian origin, took Rome and early Byzantium as its model. However, in the 6th century, it was overthrown by the Sassanians, who imposed direct rule. The Byzantines still held Lazica, and the entire region became a battleground between

◄ *This extraordinary Byzantine ivory figurine is sometimes thought to date from the 10th–13th centuries. Its purpose is unclear and nothing else like it seems to survive. The helmet with its crest and face-covering visor, the tall rectangular shield and the gaiter-like protection on the left leg could suggest a 4th-7th century date. (Bargello Mus., Florence)*

▶ *'Judgement of Solomon', in the* Commentaries of Gregory of Nazianzus, *late 9th century Byzantine. The executioner on the right has a tapering straight sword, while the guards on the left still have decorated* claves *panels on their tunics. (Bib. Nat., Ms. Gr. 510, f.215V, Paris)*

The Triumph of Constantius, mid-4th century
1: The Emperor Constantius in his gilded chariot
2: Cataphract of the Scythae regiment
3: Infantry guardsman of the Cornuti

A

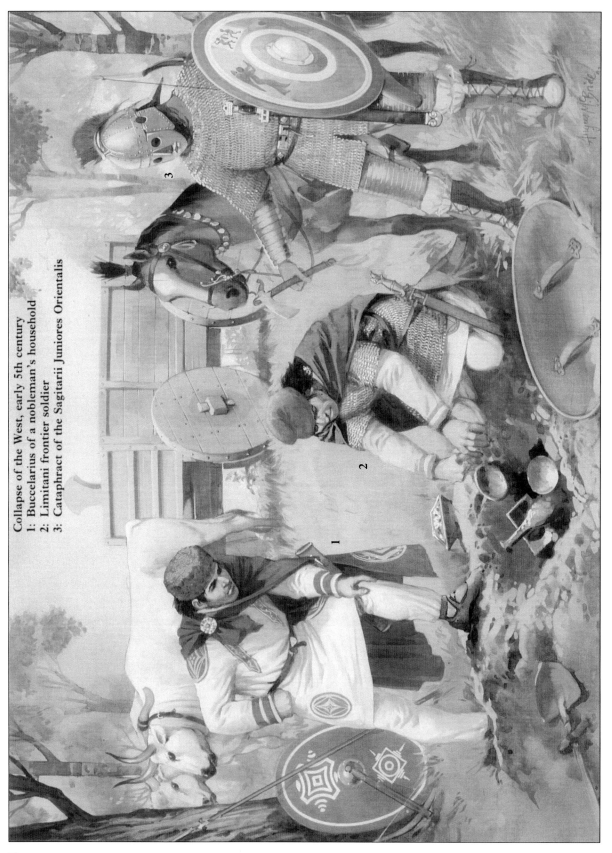

Collapse of the West, early 5th century
1: Buccelarius of a nobleman's household
2: Limitani frontier soldier
3: Cataphract of the Sagitarii Juniores Orientalis

B

Justinian's Army, 6th century
1: Thracian cavalryman of the Leones Clibanarii
2: Guards infantryman
3: Irregular of the Numerus Felicium Theodosiacus

C

Syria and the Ghassanids, 5th–6th centuries
1: Ghassanid nobleman
2: Ghassanid tribal warrior
3: Syrian nobleman from Antioch

D

Byzantine Armies of the 7th century
1: Armoured infantryman
2: Armoured cavalryman
3: Noble commander

E

The Byzantine 'Dark Age', 7th-8th centuries
1: East Anatolian peasant
2: Jacobite Abbot
3: Armenian aristocrat

F

Proclamation of an Emperor,
9th century
1: Byzantine Emperor
2: Standard bearer of
   Excubitores Guards
3a & 3b: Infantrymen

G

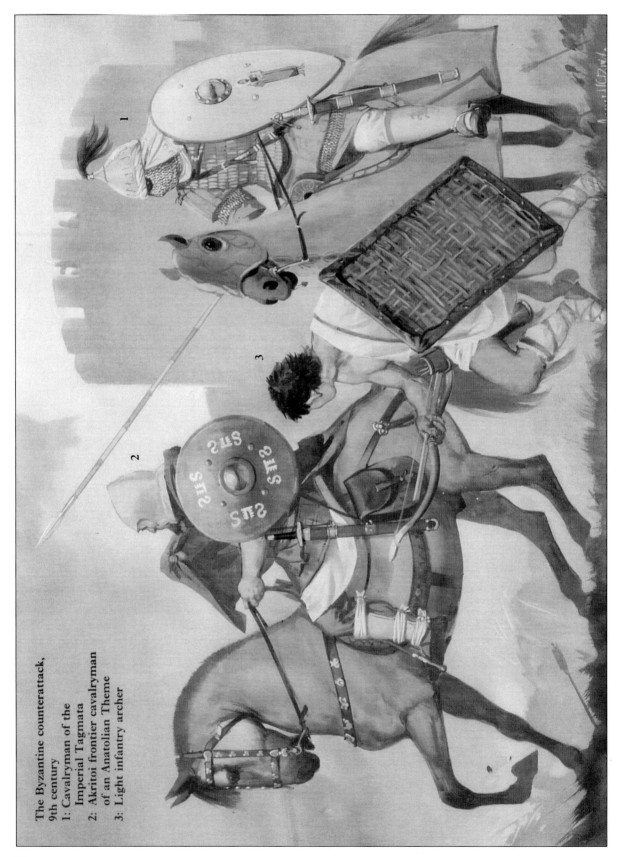

The Byzantine counterattack,
9th century
1: Cavalryman of the
   Imperial Tagmata
2: Akritoi frontier cavalryman
   of an Anatolian Theme
3: Light infantry archer

H

Byzantium and the Sassanian Empire until a short-lived Byzantium triumph in AD 627. Less than a generation later both Iberia and the northern part of Lazica, though not Abkhazia, voluntarily submitted to Muslim rule, giving the Caliphate a little-known outlet onto the Black Sea. Tblisi, which is still the capital of Georgia, now flourished as a cultural centre under Muslim princes, while there was widespread conversion to Islam. However, a Christian warrior aristocracy continued to exist, particularly in the mountains, and, like the independent Abkhazians to the north, provided mercenaries for the Byzantine army. In general, however, Georgian military effort was directed against the pro-Byzantine, anti-Muslim Khazar Turks north of the Caucasus.

Armenians

Of far greater military importance to Byzantium were the Armenians, who had a high military reputation from the 3rd to 8th centuries. The area had again been occupied by the Sassanians following a treaty with Rome in AD 363, by which time Armenia had converted to Christianity. From then on local authority was largely in the hands of a turbulent warrior aristocracy – whichever foreign empire claimed control. The aristocracy of great *ishkhans* and lesser *nakharars* lived in their own castles, imposing an early form of feudalism upon the land. The *nakharars* in particular seemed willing to fight for anyone who paid well and left them alone, or offered richer territories elsewhere. In the late 6th century Emperor Maurice cultivated these *nakharars*, encouraging many to settle around Pergamum (mod. Bergama) in western Anatolia. The importance of Armenian troops to Byzantine armies increased during the 7th century, 2,000 forming an armoured cavalry elite on the Danube frontier against the Avars, while others defended Constantinople itself.

Although Armenian troops played a prominent role in the unsuccessful Byzantine defence of Syria against the Muslim Arabs, other Armenian *nakharars* assisted the Muslim conquest of Armenia, which had itself been divided between the Sassanian and Byzantine Empires. Armenia was also the only part of

the long Byzantine–Islamic frontier not to be depopulated by war during the 8th and 9th centuries. Further south the Paulician sect, many of whom were Armenian, was crushed by the Byzantines during the same period. Some were forcibly transferred to the Balkans where they contributed to the late rise of the heretical Bogomils (see MAA 195, *Hungary and the Fall of Eastern Europe 1000–1568*), while others fled to the more tolerant atmosphere of Islam; there they served as cavalry, and were believed to regard Jesus Christ as the sun. Meanwhile their abandoned homeland was colonized by Muslims and Orthodox Armenians, starting a southward spread of Armenians which eventually brought them to the Mediterranean.

In Armenia proper two feudal principalities now emerged, the Bagratids in the north and the Artsruni in the south, with a number of mixed Arab–Armenian emirates around Lake Van, each paying tribute to the Caliphate. Under the original treaty Armenia would send 1,500 cavalry when needed. The Arab–Armenian emirates of Lake Van proved a particular thorn in the side of Byzantium before being crushed between the Byzantines, the Kurds

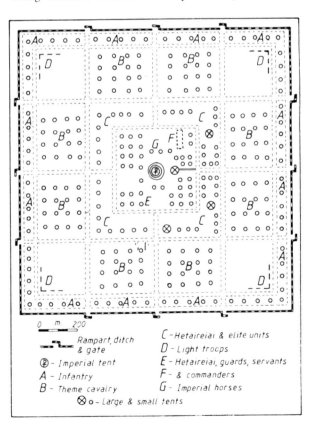

Ideal layout of an Expeditionary Camp, from a 10th century Byzantine treatise on organization and tactics (after Dennis).

0 m. 200

— Rampart, ditch & gate
Ⓟ – Imperial tent
A – Infantry
B – Theme cavalry
⊗ o – Large & small tents

C – Hetaireiai & elite units
D – Light troops
E – Hetaireiai, guards, servants
F – & commanders
G – Imperial horses

and the Hamdanid rulers of Aleppo in the 10th century. By that time some Armenians had risen to high command in Constantinople, yet a 10th century Byzantine military treatise warned darkly that Armenians made careless sentries.

Within Armenia the local rulers could theoretically raise 25,000 or even 40,000 men, but such a general levy was rare after the 7th century. Nevertheless Armenian forces remained large for their day, while the country was also very strongly fortified. Seventy castles were said to exist in the province of Vaspourakan, east of Lake Van. Villages, churches and monasteries were also fortified. In 4th century Armenia there had been a special corps of mountain troops trained to roll rocks onto their foes; while in siege warfare Armenians were equipped with iron hooks to help them scale walls, and large leather shields to protect their backs from rocks dropped from above. Military service was regarded as a privilege linked to the possession of land, and each noble led a force of free men under his own banner. All were normally mounted and were notably well equipped, Armenia being rich in iron. In fact

Armenian armour was regarded as singularly heavy, while iron horse armour was more common than elsewhere. Down-to-earth Arabic historians like Mas'udi noted that Armenian cavalry used war-axes by the 10th century, but the Armenian chronicler Stephanos Orbelian described one early 9th century rebel in more poetic terms:

'Having taken his armament and decked his superb body with a shining royal cuirass adorned with pearls, he put on a helmet topped with a tiger's head and girded his waist with a sword. Then throwing a golden shield upon his left shoulder and a strong spear in his right hand, he sprang upon his black steed and dashed at the enemy.'

Extravagant it might be, but the similarity between this hero's equipment and that of an Iranian hero in the late 10th century *Shahnamah* epic and the hero of the 12th century Georgian *Man in the Panther's Skin* epic probably reflects a common military as well as literary heritage.

One comparable Armenian epic, *David of Sassoun*, may date from the 10th century. Here Armenian horsemen play a game virtually identical to the later Turkish *cirit* or Arab *jarid*, hurling blunted javelins at each other as they career around a cavalry training ground. If this poem is indeed from the 10th century, rather than reflecting influences from later centuries of Ottoman domination, then it suggests a direct link between the ancient Roman *hippica gymnasia* cavalry training exercises, through Byzantium and Armenia, to the Turkish game of *cirit* which can still be seen in eastern Anatolia.

Kurds

The origins of the Kurds are lost in legend. One story states that they had Arab origins but broke away after a quarrel with the Ghassanids (see below). They emerge under their own name shortly before the coming of Islam, and seem to have had mixed Semitic and Armenian origins while speaking an Iranian

'Bribing guards at the gates of Gethsemane', in a 9th century Byzantine psalter. The soldiers no longer have much similarity with their late Roman predecessors. Their equipment, particularly the tall pointed helmet with a full mail aventail, shows Central Asian Turkish or Iranian influence. The warriors also have mail hauberks, long spears and small shields slung behind their shoulders. (Monastery of the Pantocrator, Ms. no. 61, f. 89r, Mount Athos)

language. The Kurds then gradually rose to prominence under their own petty princes from the 7th to 10th centuries. Politically and militarily almost all their activities were within the Muslim sphere, only being directly involved with Byzantium after the Byzantine Empire conquered eastern Anatolia in the 10th and 11th centuries.

Arab Ghassanids

Along Rome's northern frontiers Germanic tribal *foederati* settled in areas inhabited by Celts and other non-Germanic peoples. In the Middle East, however, Arab *foederati* took military control of lands which had already long been inhabited by Arabs or other Semites. Unlike earlier Roman vassal kingdoms, such as the Jewish Herodians or Arab Nabateans, these new *foederati* rarely fought each other, because only one tribal group was permitted to provide frontier governors or *phylarchs* at one time. Nevertheless these *phylarchs* did wage war on their own account, clashing with tribes of the deep desert or with the pro-Sassanian Lakhmids of the Iraqi frontier. There could also be trouble within the frontier tribes, often directed against a leadership which was seen as growing too Romanized or unsufficiently generous with the donations paid by Romano-Byzantine authorities. Yet *phylarchs* and *foederati* did tend to settle and accept the more civilized life of Syria.

In summer the Ghassanid leadership lived in villages in agreement with village leaders, just as Syrian and Jordanian bedouin do today. The fortifications of Ghassanid 'palaces' along the desert frontier were for show rather than for real, yet some had small barracks nearby for the *phylarchs*' own guards. The Ghassanids also founded numerous towns and villages, reception halls, forts and markets as well as churches and monasteries within and beyond the Imperial frontiers. As protectors of the Syriac-Jacobite church they were, however, regarded as heretics by the Orthodox Byzantines. Meanwhile St. Sergius was the patron of Arab nomad Christians, his church at Jabiya on the Golan Heights becoming a centre of pilgrimage.

The *phylarch* and a Roman *dux* shared responsibility for a specific length of frontier, the Ghassanid *phylarch* commanding local *foederati* led by native officers. These forces lived partly within the *limes*

'Chaldeans stealing Job's camels and slaying his servants', 9th century Byzantine manuscript. The Chaldeans, who may be shown as warriors of the eastern frontier region, are armed with a spear, maces and weapons with curved blades and long handles. These could be an early attempt to portray curved sabres. (Vatican Lib., Cod. Gr. 749, f.19r, Rome)

while controlling the tribes beyond it. The *phylarch* also received a handsome subsidy and his *foederati* were paid a regular *annona* allowance. During the early Byzantine period this system proved effective and relatively cheap. By the 6th century Byzantium's regular troops had handed much of the old *limes* over to the *phylarchs*, but in response to the growing power of the pro-Sassanian Lakhmids on the Iraqi side of the desert, Justinian placed the various *phylarchs* under a new Ghassanid monarchy responsible for the entire frontier from the Euphrates to the Gulf of Aqaba. To the Romano-Byzantines this super-*phylarch* lacked true independence, but to the Arabs the Ghassanid *bitriq* 'patrician' appeared as a great Arab king.

In open battle Ghassanid and other Arab horsemen were rarely able to stand against heavily armoured Sassanian cavalry. Yet they were valuable enough to be used far from their own territory, Heraclius taking his Arab allies as far north as Azerbayjan on the Caspian Sea. In the south, where there was only a limited threat from Arabian tribes, *phylarchs* were treated differently, being responsible for internal security. One, for example, put down a number of anti-Christian revolts by the Samaritans of Palestine. Arab nomad tribes in Sinai may have similarly been paid to help Byzantine *condomae* guard the caravan routes between Syria and Egypt.

'The arrest of David', in a 9th century Byzantine psalter. The soldiers appear to be equipped as light cavalry with rounded helmets, long spears, small shields on the shoulder, and a long straight-bladed sword. (Monastery of the Pantocrator, Ms. no. 61, f. 68v, Mount Athos)

This system was shattered by the Sassanian occupation of Syria and Egypt in the early 7th century. Loyalty to Byzantium was shaken, particularly among the bedouin, and a generation grew up without experiencing Romano-Byzantine rule. Meanwhile Sassanian authority was itself weak, resulting in insecurity and raiding. Even after Byzantine forces retook Syria they made no effort to go beyond the Dead Sea, abandoning southern Palestine, southern and eastern Jordan and much of the Sinai. Towns such as Aila (mod. Aqaba) now lay beyond the Byzantine frontier, and seem to have been governed by local bishops who made their own agreements with neighbouring tribes. Similar arrangements were even made by some towns within the Empire. On the other hand the Byzantines were rebuilding a coalition of allies around the Qudama

tribe of Jordan and the northern Hijaz at the time the Prophet Muhammad was creating his confederation of Muslim tribes further south. Christian Ghassanid troops fought for Byzantium at the decisive battle of Yarmouk in AD 636 where Romano-Byzantine power was broken for ever. Ghassanids also defended the Syrian capital of Damascus against the Muslims in AD 634. But they did not use the ancient *castellum*; rather they built a small new tower and attempted to protect the city from a base camp at Marj Rahit to the east.

Berbers

In North Africa some Berber tribes forged long-standing alliances with the Romans and Byzantines, the Musulami proving perhaps the most reliable. Other *limitanai* were recruited from both sides of an ill-defined and changing Roman frontier. The military organization of such pro-Roman auxiliaries is better known than that of other more recalcitrant tribes, but probably did not differ much from them (see MAA 243, *Rome's Enemies (5): The Desert Frontier*). At first they were led by, or were at least under the nominal authority of, Roman officers; but by the 5th century the *praepositi* who commanded local *gentili* tribal militias were themselves of local origin. These senior men also controlled small *castra* forts, many having their own arsenals, in which the Berber irregulars were based. Most late Roman or Byzantine Berber auxiliaries fought as cavalry and assisted in regional defence, as well as sending units to the regular army elsewhere. In return the Imperial Army lent a few regulars to serve the more important Berber princes, and sent elaborate gifts to reinforce the prestige of allied leaders. By the 7th century, however, the pro-Byzantine Berber tribes were operating 'up country', largely in the hills, and seem to have been virtually cut off from the remaining Byzantine coastal garrisons.

Further Reading

In recent years there has been a revival of interest in the Fall of the Roman Empire and the survival of Byzantium; hence the following list is longer than usual. Even so, readers should also see the *Further Reading* sections in *Attila and the Nomad Hordes* (Elite 30) and *Rome's Enemies (5): The Desert Frontier* (MAA 243).

F. Aussaresses, *L'Armée Byzantine à fin du VIe Siècle* (Paris 1909).

N. J. E. Austin, *Ammianus on Warfare: An Investigation into Ammianus' Military Knowledge* (Brussels 1979).

N. H. Baynes, 'The Military Operations of the Emperor Heraclius', *United Services Magazine* XLVI–XLVII (1913).

M. C. Bishop (edit.), *The Production and Distribution of Roman Military Equipment* (BAR Internat. Series 275, Oxford 1985).

A. D. H. Bivar, 'Cavalry Equipment and Tactics on the Euphrates Frontier', *Dumbarton Oaks Papers* XXVI (1972).

A. E. R. Boak, *Manpower shortage and the Fall of the Roman Empire* (Ann Arbor 1955).

A. E. R. Boak, *The Master of the Offices in the Later Roman and Byzantine Empires* (London 1919).

J. C. Coulston (edit.), *Military Equipment and the Identity of Roman Soldiers* (BAR Internat. Series 394, Oxford 1988).

G. T. Dennis, 'Byzantine Battle Flags', *Byzantinische Forschungen VIII* (1982).

G. T. Dennis, *Three Byzantine Military Treatises* (Washington 1985).

C. Diehl, *L'Afrique Byzantine: Histoire de la Domination Byzantine (533–709)* (Paris 1896).

L. Fauber, *Narses, Hammer of the Goths: The Life and Times of Narses the Eunuch* (New York 1990).

A. Ferrill, *The Fall of the Roman Empire: The Military Explanation* (London 1986).

C. Foss & D. Winfield, *Byzantine Fortifications; an introduction* (Pretoria 1986).

C. Foss, *History and Archaeology of Byzantine Asia Minor* (London 1990).

R. I. Frank, 'Scholae Palatinae: The Palace Guards of the Later Roman Empire', *Papers and Monographs of the American Academy in Rome XXIII* (1969).

L. A. Garcia Moreno, 'Organizacion militar de Bisancio en la Peninsula Iberica, ss. VI–VII', *Hispania CXXIII* (1973).

P. Goubert, *Byzance avant l'Islam*, 2 vols. (Paris 1951 & 1965).

D. F. Graf, 'The Saracens and the Defence of the Arabian Frontier', *Bulletin of the American Schools of Oriental Research CCIX* (1978).

M. Grant, *The Fall of the Roman Empire – a reappraisal* (Annenberg 1976).

A. Guillou, *Studies in Byzantine Italy* (London 1970).

J. F. Haldon, *Byzantine Praetorians: An Administrative, Institutional and Social Survey of the Opsikion and Tagmata c. 580–900* (Bonn 1984).

J. F. Haldon, *Recruitment and Conscription in the Byzantine Army c. 550–950: A Study of the Origins of the Stratiotika Ktemata* (Vienna 1979).

J. F. Haldon, 'Some Aspects of Byzantine Military Technology from the Sixth to the Tenth Centuries', *Byzantine and Modern Greek Studies I* (1975).

D. Haupt & H. G. Horn (edits.), *Studien zu den Militärgrenzen Roms, II* (Cologne 1977).

D. J. F. Hill, 'Some Notes on Archery in the Roman World', *Journal of the Society of Archer-Antiquaries I* (1958).

D. Hoffmann, *Das spätromische Bewegungsheer und die Notitia Dignitatum* (Cologne 1969).

S. James, 'Evidence from Dura Europos for the Origins of Late Roman Helmets', *Syria LXIII* (1986).

A. H. M. Jones, *The Later Roman Empire, 284–602 AD* (Oxford 1964).

W. E. Kaegi, *Army, Society and Religion in Byzantium* (London 1982).

'Death of Absolom', in a Byzantine manuscript of c. AD 860. Although the animal is a donkey or mule, its saddle is clearly of the medieval wood-framed type with a raised pommel and swept back cantle. (Chludov Psalter, f. 140v, Historical Museum, Ms. Add. Gr. 129, Moscow)

W. E. Kaegi, *Byzantine Military Unrest 471–843: An Interpretation* (Amsterdam 1981).

H. Klumback (edit.), *Spärromische Gardehelme* (Munich 1973).

T. Kollias, *Byzantinischen Waffen* (Vienna 1988).

T. Kollias, 'Zaba, Zabareion, Zabareiotis', *Jahrbuch der österreichischen Byzantinistik XXIX* (1980).

C. P. Kyrris, 'Military Colonies in Cyprus in the Byzantine Period: Their Character, Purpose and Extent', *Byzantinoslavica XXXI* (1970).

J. Laurent, *Études d'Histoire Arménienne* (Louvain 1971).

P. Llewellyn, *Rome in the Dark Ages* (London 1971).

E. W. Marsden, *Greek and Roman Artillery: Technical Treatises* (Oxford 1971).

S. Mitchell (edit.), *Armies and Frontiers in Roman and Byzantine Anatolia* (BAR Internat. Series 156, Oxford 1983).

D. Nishamura, 'Crossbows, Arrow-Guides and the Solenarion', *Byzantion LVIII* (1988).

S. T. Parker (edit.), *The Roman Frontier in Central Jordan: Interim Report on the 'Limes Arabicus' Project, 1980–1985* (BAR Internat. Series 340/II, Oxford 1987).

P. Partner, *the Lands of St. Peter* (London 1972).

H. Pasdermadjian, *Histoire de l'Arménie* (Paris 1964).

G. Ravegnani, *Soldati di Bisanzio in Età Giustiniana* (Rome 1988).

P. Schreiner, 'Zur Ausrüstung des Kriegers in Byzanz, im Kiewer Russland und in Nordeuropa', *Acta Universitatis Upsaliensis, Figura ns XIX* (1981).

O. Seeck (trans.), *Notitia Dignitatum* (Berlin 1876).

A. N. Stratos *Byzantium in the Seventh Century*, 5 vols. (Amsterdam 1968–1980).

J. L. Teall, 'The Barbarians in Justinian's Armies', *Speculum XI* (1965).

R. Tomlin, 'The Late-Roman Empire', in *Warfare in the Ancient World*, edit. J. Hackett (London 1989).

A. A. Vasiliev, *Byzance et les Arabes I* (Brussels 1934), *II* (Brussels 1950).

M. Whitby, *The Emperor Maurice and his Historian: Theophylact Simocatta on Persian and Balkan Warfare* (Oxford 1988).

J. E. Wiita, *The Ethnika in Byzantine Military Treatises* (University Microfilms, Ann Arbor 1978).

THE PLATES

A: The Triumph of Constantius, mid-4th century:

A1: The Emperor Constantius in his gilded chariot

Written and visual sources show that late Roman Emperors continued to wear ceremonial armour and regalia based on antique forms; yet there were subtle changes. Here Constantius has a gold diadem instead of a victor's laurel wreath, and his cloak is secured by a Germanic brooch. His cuirass of tiny bronze scales is worn over a soft red leather 'arming jerkin' from which fringed *pteruges* hang at shoulders and waist. His magnificent gilded iron helmet is a late Roman type, but he still carries a symbolic gilded spear as a mark of authority. (Main sources: bronze statue of an Emperor, mid-4 cent, *in situ* Barletta; carved reliefs on Arch of Constantine, early 4 cent, *in situ* Rome; bust of a late Roman Emperor, late 4–early 5 cents, Louvre Museum, Paris.) The chariot is based on carvings on the Arch of Constantine in Rome, as is the driver.

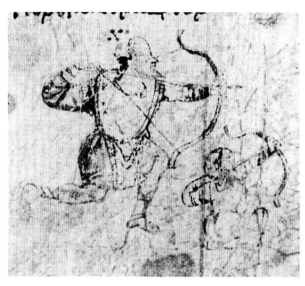

'The wicked bend their bows (Psalm 10)', in a Byzantine manuscript of c. AD 860. With their composite bows and thumb-draw style of shooting, these unarmoured men probably reflect Byzantine light infantry. (Chludov Psalter, f. 18v, Historical Museum, Ms. Add. Gr. 129, Moscow)

A2: Cataphract of the Scythae regiment, early–mid-4th century

The appearance of late Roman armoured cavalry had little in common with earlier Roman horsemen. This trooper has a segmented iron helmet of good quality, a cuirass of bronze scales riveted directly to one another, a long cavalry *spatha* sword and a shorter *gladius*. The dragon standard was of Central Asian origin, perhaps introduced to Rome by the Scythians. His saddle is of a new, perhaps partially wood-framed type but still lacks stirrups. Experts have suggested that this saddle actually provided less support than the earlier Roman four-horned saddle and that its adoption made little sense unless accompanied by stirrups which, for some reason, later Roman artists may not have shown. (Main sources: helmet, 4 cent, Rijksmuseum, Leiden; copy of lost early 4 cent wall paintings in Luxor, Bodleian Lib., Ms. Wilk. XXII, Oxford; armour from Dura Europos, 3 cent, Yale Univ. Art Gall., New Haven; relief carvings, early 4 cent, *in situ* Arch of Constantine, Rome; silver horse-collar from Rome, 4 cent, Brit. Mus., nr. 66.12–29.25, London)

A3: Infantry guardsman of the Cornuti, early–mid-4th century

In complete contrast to the cavalryman, this foot soldier only has a highly decorated helmet and a large shield to protect him, reversing the situation in earlier Roman armies. In addition to a standard with a silver-gilt figure of Victory, he carries two light *verutum* javelins and a lead-weighted, arrow-flighted *plumbatum*. (Main sources: relief carvings, early 4 cent, *in situ* Arch of Constantine, Rome; helmet from Augsburg-Pfersee, 4–5 cents, Germ. Nat. Museum, inv. W.1943, Nurnberg; buckle, brooch & knife from Oudenburg fort near Ostend, after Mertens)

B: Collapse in the West, early 5th century:
B1: Buccelarius of a nobleman's household, early 5th century

The appearance of those armed retainers who formed 'private armies' shortly before the collapse of the Roman Empire would have varied according to the wealth and whim of their paymasters. This man wears a flat-topped fur cap fashionable in the 4th–5th centuries while his tunic has embroidered bands and patches or *claves* associated with military status in Byzantine times. In addition to a substantial hunting spear he has a small hunting crossbow. Some military theorists advocated its use in battle, but whether Roman troops ever used them during the final chaotic years is unknown. (Main sources: mosaics, early 4 cent, *in situ* Piazza Armerina, Sicily; carved reliefs of crossbows, 2–3 cents, Mus. Crozatier, Le Puy; spearhead from grave in Amiens, 4 cent, after Massy)

B2: Limitani frontier soldier, mid-5th century

The *limitanii* had almost disappeared by the time the Western Roman Empire collapsed in the mid-5th century. What little is known indicates that they now formed local militias, probably with only rudimentary equipment. This man is fortunate in possessing a mail shirt of a type which would remain in use until the 12th century. His soft leather cap was typical of the period and his trousers are tied up below the knees as seen in pictorial sources. His sword, which has been made with a cast bronze 'bird-headed' hilt, may well be a family heirloom. The construction and design show it to be at least a century old. (Main sources: *Virgilius Vaticana*, early 5 cent. Vat. Lib., Ms. Lat. 3225, Rome; *Virgilius Romanus*, late 5 cent, Vat. Lib., Ms. Lat. 3867, Rome.) The ox-cart, with coloured patches perhaps for identification, is based upon early 4th century mosaics in the Piazza Armerina, Sicily.

B3: Cataphract of the Sagitarii Juniores Orientalis, early 5th century

Even less is known about the appearance of 5th century Roman cavalry. Pictures are few, stylized and archaic, or exist only in later copies. Written sources

Marginal from a 9th century Byzantine Bible. In this simple illustration armour appears to be based upon classical Roman prototypes, yet it may still reflect the equipment of some elite guard units in Constantinople. (Bib. Nat., Ms. Gr. 923, f.107v, Paris)

tend to be unclear or written by men advocating change rather than describing what existed. Much of this trooper's kit is, therefore, based on deduction. The helmet, for example, is comparable to those in various mosaics and may be the Roman prototype of the famous Anglo-Saxon Sutton Hoo helmet. Face-masks certainly appeared on lost carvings recorded only in later drawings, although a few undated masks were found in the Great Palace in Constantinople, as was a decorated axe. Mail shirts were a common protection, while the laminated arm defences are an interpretation of recorded carvings, based on Central Asian armours of a century later. The laminated leg defences are similarly an interpretation of lost carvings, though they are also based upon flimsy bronze leg pieces which may have been a parade armour. Even the archery equipment has to be based on unclear manuscripts; but his sword is a new form common in the graves of Germanic invaders. Not surprisingly the horse's bridle reflect strong Central Asian influence, though this is confirmed by carvings. (Main sources; axe, 4 cent, Dumbarton Oaks Coll.,

Washington; bronze Roman leg armour, Mus. of Antiq., Edinburgh; drawing of lost c. AD 400 Column of Arcadius, Trinity Coll. Lib., Cambridge; later copy of early 5 cent *Notitia Dignitatum*, Staatsbib., Ms. Lat. 10.291, Munich; 'Story of Abraham' on mosaics. AD 432–440, *in situ* Santa Maria Maggiore, Rome; *Virgilius Vaticana*, early 5 cent, Vat. Lib. Ms. Lat. 3225, Rome)

C: Justinian's Army, 6th century:
C1: Thracian cavalryman of the Leones Clibanarii, late 6th century

The few surviving illustrations of fully equipped soldiers from Justinian's time tend to be less stylized than the art of a century before. Written descriptions are also more factual. This man has a segmented *spangenhelm* of Italo-Germanic form. His lamellar cuirass shows strong Turco-Central Asian influence, as does his archery equipment. The very long sword on his hip was common to Iranian and steppe cavalry and was probably adopted by Romano-Byzantine horsemen. Written descriptions of Byzantine horse-armour show that the models on which it was based were Turkish and Iranian in origin, although no pictures of early examples of Byzantine horse-armour survive. (Main sources: helmet from Batajnica, 5–6 cents, Archaeol. Mus., Zagreb; harness & weapons from necropolis at Nocera Umbra, 6–7 cents, Mus. dell'Alto Medioevo, Rome; *Isola Rizza Dish* showing armoured rider, 6–7 cents, Castelvecchio Mus., Verona)

C2: Guards infantryman, mid-6th century

A detailed representation of Justinian's bodyguard on the mosaics of San Vitale in Ravenna has them unarmoured, except for shields and spears. To equip these men for war one has to look elsewhere, and the result suggests plumed helmets of late Roman segmented construction, perhaps with a cloth-covered

The 'Forty Martyrs' on a Cappadocian wall painting of the mid-10th century probably give a much clearer impression of the equipment, costume and horse harness used by Byzantine frontier armies than does finer art from the Imperial capital. Here a variety of arms and armour is shown, including single and double-edged straight swords, a cuirass of probably hardened leather scales (left centre) and perhaps linen-covered felt or leather cuirasses (right & centre right). (In situ, Dovecote Church at Cavusin, AD 963–969, Turkey; author's photograph)

coif or aventail and a mail hauberk. Here a guardsman retains the magnificently decoratd shield of the San Vitale mosaics. Neck torques were also worn and survived in Egyptian representations of military saints for centuries after the Muslim conquest. (Main sources: 'Siege of the Citadel of Faith', 6 cent Coptic wood carving, Konig. Mus., inv. I.4782, Berlin, lost during World War II; 'David and Goliath', carved limestone relief from Egypt, 6 cent, Coptic Mus., Cairo; 'St. Menas' in full armour, page from Coptic hymnal, 6–8 cents, John Rylands Lib., Ms. S.33, Manchester; axe from Butrint, 6–8 cents Albania, after Anamali; 'Guards of Justinian', mid-6 cent mosaic, *in situ* church of San Vitale, Ravenna)

C3: Irregular of the Numerus Felicium Theodosiacus, 6th century

This light infantryman represents the bulk of 6th century Byzantine armies. Shorts are clearly illustrated in mosaics of the period. His body protection is a type frequently shown in Byzantine art from the 6th century onwards. Its construction is unknown but has here been interpreted as soft armour of layered felt. He is armed with a sword of Hunnish derivation. (Main sources: 'Hunting scenes' on mosaic from the Great Palace of Constantinople, Mosaics Museum, Istanbul; *Cotton Genesis*, 6 cent manuscript made in Constantinople, Brit. Lib., Cod. Otho B. BI, f.19v, London; 'Guard of Saul' on *David Plates*, early 7 cent Byzantine silver from Cyprus, Met. Mus., New York)

The Porta Nigra, 'Black Gate', of Trier in Germany. Erected at the start of the 4th century, it formed part of the fortress of a city which served as the Imperial capital in the last decades of the Western Empire. (Author's photograph)

D: Syria and the Ghassanids, 5th–6th centuries:
D1: Ghassanid nobleman, 6th century

Ghassanid forces were largely equipped from Byzantine arsenals. This Arab nobleman has a late Roman helmet and a mail hauberk which includes a mail coif, as shown in late Roman sources. His sword also appears in early Byzantine art, though no surviving examples are known. The red and white banner is based on a description of a Ghassanid tribal flag from a century later. The only other specifically Arab feature is this man's long hair. (Main sources: relief carving of early Ghassanid warrior from Rushaydeh, 5–6 cents, Local Mus., Suwaidah, Syria; *David Plates*, early 7 cent Byzantine silver from

Cyprus, Met. Mus., New York; 6 cent mosaics, *in situ* Church of Deacon Thomas, Mount Nebo, Jordan; 6 cent. mosaics, *in situ* Church of Ippolito, Madaba, Jordan)

D2: Ghassanid tribal warrior, 6th century

Only this man's early Byzantine helmet reflects his role as an Imperial ally. Otherwise he wears the *izar* cloth wound around his body typical of pre-Islamic Arab tribesmen. His large simple bow is also typically Arabian, as are his sandals and his shield of interwoven palm stems. (Main sources: helmet from Hadithah, 6–early 7 cents, Kerak Castle Mus., Jordan; Arab nomad warrior on 6 cent mosaic, *in situ* Monastery of Kayanos, Mount Nebo, Jordan)

D3: Syrian nobleman from Antioch, 5th–6th centuries

This member of Antioch's social elite may be a member of the 'Blues' Circus Faction. He has the front and sides of his head shaved 'in the Hun fashion' criticized by at least one Syrian churchman. His mid-length trousers may have been a short-lived fashion; his powerful composite bow, here used for hunting, was far more effective than the longbow used by the Ghassanid Arab tribesman. The saddle has a pommel at the front but no cantle at the back, a feature reflecting Iranian influence. (Main sources: 6–early 7 cent mosaics from Harbiye & Antioch, Art Mus., Worcester Mass.; late 6 cent mosaic, *in situ* Chapel of Martyr Theodore, Madaba, Jordan; mid-6 cent mosaic, *in situ* Church of Deacon Thomas, Mount Nebo, Jordan; 6 cent mosaic, *in situ* Church of Martyrs Lot and Procopius, Madaba, Jordan)

E: Byzantine armies of the 7th century:
E1: Armoured infantryman, 7th century

The 7th century was another period from which few illustrations survive. The best-equipped infantry appear to have had short-sleeved mail hauberks and remarkably large shields, plus spears and swords. This man's helmet is based upon one found in Central Europe which may be of Byzantine form. The addition of a mail aventail is hypothetical, reflecting a high degree of Turkish and specifically Avar influence. His sword is based upon an unusual Scandinavian form which is itself likely to reflect Byzantine origins. (Main sources: 7–8 cent helmets from Prag-Stromovska, Nat. Mus., Prague; 'St. Menas' fully armed, on page from a 6–8 cent Coptic hymnal, John Rylands Lib., Ms. S.33, Manchester; 'David and Goliath', 7–8 cent wall painting, *in situ* Chapel III, Bawit, Egypt; ivory panels of military saints on *Pulpit of Henry II*, 7–8 cent Coptic, Aachen Cathedral; *David Plates*, early 7 cent Byzantine silver from Cyprus, Met. Mus. of Art, New York; soldier at martyrdom scene, early 7 cent wall painting, *in situ* Santa Maria Antiqua, Rome; 6 cent sword from Kragehul bog, Denmark, after Oakeshott)

E2: Armoured cavalryman, early 7th century

This trooper has been given a plumed cap over his helmet, as worn by warriors from Iran and the

The restored Edirne (Adrianople) gate in the walls of Istanbul (Constantinople). These defences defied invaders for over a thousand years. (Author's photograph)

Caucasus. This could be the explanation for some of the otherwise extraordinary outlines of many helmets seen in 7th–9th century Byzantine art. The massive padded gorget around the man's neck is a hypothetical reconstruction based on written descriptions. Turkish and Avar influence can be seen on the belt, sword and bowcase, as shown by surviving fragments and pictorial sources. (Main sources: *David Plates*, early 7 cent Byzantine silver from Cyprus, Met. Mus. of Art, New York; carved ivory plaque showing armoured horseman, 7 cent from Nocera Umbra, Mus. dell'Alto Medioevo, Rome; sheath, shield fragments & spurs from Castel Trosino, 7–8 cents, Mus. Dell'Alto Medioevo, Rome)

E3: Noble commander, late 7th century

One remarkable and recently discovered fragment of wall painting sheds light on the costume of the 7th century Byzantine elite though not, unfortunately, on their military equipment. A long tunic with richly embroidered *claves* and three-quarter sleeves was worn over a long-sleeved shirt, either with soft riding boots or, as here, with highly decorated shoes indicating high status. The practice of impaling the head and hands of a defeated rebel, presumably as a warning to others, seems to have been common in Byzantium at this time. (Main sources: 'Procession of a victorious Emperor', wall painting of 7–8 cents, *in situ* Church of Hagios Demetrios, Thessaloniki; 'Archangel Gabriel in full armour', wax-painted wooden panel, 6–7 cent Egypt, Coptic Mus., inv. 9083, Cairo; decorated shield boss from Nocera Umbra, Italo-Byzantine 7 cent, Mus. dell'Alto Medioevo, Rome)

F: The Byzantine 'Dark Age', 7th–8th centuries:
F1: East Anatolian peasant, 7th century
With the collapse of the Empire's eastern frontier in the 7th century and the Muslim conquest of most of Armenia, Byzantine resistance became a war of ambush and raiding. The mountain folk of eastern Anatolia, Armenians and others, served as guides and irregulars to all sides. Their huge bear- or sheepskin cloaks protected them from the fierce weather and perhaps also acted as a form of armour. The peasants of this area are sometimes depicted with long-bladed, long-handled weapon. It could be a misrepresentation of a dagger or early sabre, or it could be a real weapon from which some later medieval staff weapons developed. Sturdy pack donkeys were the main beasts of burden in the precipitous mountains of eastern Anatolia, and this elaborate pack-saddle continued to be used from late Roman times throughout the Middle Ages. (Main sources: carved reliefs, Armenian c. AD 640, *in situ* Mren Cathedral; carved reliefs of tribute bearers, c. AD 390, *in situ* Column base of Theodosius, Istanbul; 16 cent drawing of lost Column of Theodosius, c. AD 390, Louvre Mus., Paris; *Vienna Genesis*, 6 cent Syria, Nat. Bib., Ms. Theol. Gr. 31, Vienna)

F2: Jacobite Abbot, 7th–8th centuries
The monasteries of eastern Anatolia served as islands of refuge in a turbulent period; but they also got caught up in the fighting, serving as fortified bases for one side or the other. Orthodox establishments naturally supported the Empire; Armenian monas-

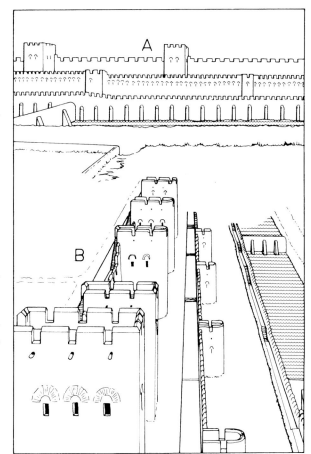

Reconstructed views of the land walls of Constantinople. (A) from outside the city; (B) looking south (after Meyer-Plath & Schneider).

teries looked after their own people; Nestorians tended to support the Muslims; while Jacobites found themselves in the middle of many conflicts. Although almost all monks and abbots wore black each sect had its own subtle differences, many of which are still reflected in the ecclesiastic dress of present-day Middle Eastern churches. Here a Jacobite abbot wears a decorated hood, whereas a Nestorian might already have adopted a black turban. (Main sources: ceramic 'wine jar' painted with picture of a monk, 9 cent Iraq from Samarra, present location unknown; lustre painted jar, 10 cent Iraq, Freer Gall. of Art, Washington; lustre painted bowl, early 12 cent Egypt, Victoria & Albert Mus., London; frontispiece of volume of *Kitab al Aghani*, early 13 cent Iraq, Nat. Lib., Ms. Farsi 579/4, Cairo; relief carvings, 13 cent, *in situ* Monastery of Mar Behnam, near Mosul)

The south-eastern walls of Thessaloniki. They date from the late 4th century and lead up to a massive circular tower built in the early Ottoman period. (Author's photograph)

F3: Armenian aristocrat, 7th–8th centuries

Apart from the magnificence of his clothes, this man is equipped as an ordinary Armenian light cavalryman. His large cap was originally an Iranian fashion but was adopted by many Middle Eastern and Caucasian peoples from the 7th century. In fact much of his costume and his weaponry reflects the Iranian and early Turkish fashions that would become common throughout the area. The belt, for example, was of Central Asian origin but came to be the mark of military aristocracies in many countries. The horse's saddle has a raised, though now clearly wooden pommel but no cantle. Stirrups have also been adopted. (Main sources: relief carvings, c. AD 600–650, Georgian, *in situ* Church of the Holy Cross, Mtzkhet'a; carved reliefs, Armenian c. AD 640, *in situ* Mren Cathedral; *David Plates*, early 7 cent Byzantine silverware, Met. Mus. of Art, New York)

G: Proclamation of an Emperor, 9th century:
G1: Byzantine Emperor, 9th century

The ceremonial dress of a Byzantine Emperor had changed from that of his Roman predecessors. His role as a Christian leader now predominated and was reflected in extravagantly decorated costume based upon that of a priest. The early diadem has become a crown. Over a three-quarter sleeved silk *dalmatic* is a long strip of heavily embroidered fabric known as a *pallium*. Over this he would wear a *maniakion* cloak which, probably being of Persian origin, was not an ecclesiastical garment. The small spear, symbolizing his power, and his pearl-studded boots were the only other non-religious items. (Main sources: mounted Emperor on silk fabric. 8–9 cents, Textile Mus., Lyons; 'elevation on an Emperor' in *Chludov Psalter*, c. AD 860, Ms. Add. Gr. 129, Hist. Mus., Moscow; 'Emperor Constantine VII' on carved ivory plaque, c. AD 945, Victoria & Albert Mus., London)

G2: Standard-bearer of Excubitores Guards, 8th–9th centuries

Central Asian and Iranian–Islamic influence now dominated Byzantine military equipment. Byzantine art still portrayed warriors in archaic, pseudo-Roman gear but other illustrations seem closer to reality. Very few pieces of arms or armour survive from Byzantium itself, though fragments from the Kuban area on the north-eastern coast of the Black Sea close to Byzantine-ruled Crimea and Byzantine-influenced Georgia, may be of Byzantine origin. His directly riveted segmented helmet, with its hanging mail aventail, could be a Byzantine variation on a common Turco-Islamic form. The lamellar cuirass was worn by elite Byzantine troops and sometimes seems to have been partially covered by a 'shirt' which could have served as a kind of regimental uniform. Gauntlets were reserved for standard bearers and marines.

Porta San Sebastiano, Rome, photographed before the Via Appia in the foreground was cleared. The basic gate was built by Honorius in the late 4th or early 5th century. The tall half-round towers date from around AD 500, while the entire structure was repaired by Justinian's general Belisarius in the 6th century. (Archivio Fotografico, Touring Club d'Italia)

Greaves to protect the legs are mentioned but are not identifiable in the artistic record; the ones shown here are based upon fragments from the Kuban area, said to date from the 8th century. (Main sources: *Chludov Psalter*, c. AD 860, Ms. Add. Gr. 129, Hist. Mus., Moscow; *Byzantine Psalter*, 9 cent, Mon. of Pantocrator, Ms. 61, Mount Athos; helmet and greaves fragments from near Tuapse, Kuban area 8 cent, Hist. Mus., Moscow; helmet from Novorosijsk, Kuban area 9 cent, Local Mus., Novorosijsk)

G3a & 3b: Infantrymen, 8th–9th centuries

Byzantine infantry varied considerably in their equipment and costume. Most appear to have been unarmoured, though helmets were reasonably common, as were straight double-edged swords. Axes with half-moon blades were probably based on the Islamic *najikh*. Spears were by far the most common weapon; while shields varied in size, decoration and construction. There are references to ones made of wood, leather and even iron, though the latter probably referred to large bosses rather than an entirely metal construction. (Main sources: *Chludov Psalter*, c. AD 860, Ms. Add. Gr. 129, Hist. Mus., Moscow; *Byzantine Psalter*, 9 cent, Mon. of Pantocrator, Ms. 61, Mount Athos)

H: The Byzantine counterattack, 9th century:
H1: Cavalryman of the Imperial Tagmata, 9th century

There was a clear division in quality and perhaps style of equipment between the elite Imperial units around Constantinople, and *theme* or regional armies. This magnificently equipped cavalryman is again based on a mixture of stylized pictorial sources and more detailed written evidence. There seem to be virtually no surviving pieces of Byzantine military gear from this period, except for a slightly later mail shirt and shield boss, a handful of buckles, and some Balkan weaponry of possible Byzantine origin. The horse's *chamfron* head protection is based upon a unique recently discovered example from Sudan which almost certainly had a Muslim-Egyptian origin. Written sources strongly suggest that Egyptian and Syrian armies were very similar to those of Byzantium. The decorative features and colours of this man's kit are largely based on the *Digenes Akritas* epic poem which may have been written close to the Syrian border in the 10th century. The saint painted on his shield is, however, mentioned in an Arabic account of a fight between Muslim and Byzantine champions. This Imperial cavalryman has a segmented helmet decorated with a pseudo-Arabic inscrip-

The deserted town of Risafa, in the Syrian Desert south of the Euphrates. It was strongly fortified by the Emperor Justinian in the early 6th century and later became a major residence of the Arab Ghassanids, Byzantium's phylarchs on the frontier facing the Iranians. (Author's photograph)

tion and a face-protecting mail aventail. His small lamellar cuirass is over a quilted *epilorikon*, the long sleeves of which have been laced up to expose part of a mail hauberk. In addition to the bronze *chamfron*, the horse is protected by a *bard* of glued and stitched layers of felt. (Main sources: *chamfron* from Soba, 8–14 cents Sudan, Nat. Mus., Khartoum; gilded bronze shield-boss, 10–11 cents, Archaeol. Mus., Aleppo; mail shirt, 10 cent, Archaeol. Mus., Sofia; 'Joshua' on late 10 cent wall painting, *in situ* Mon. of Osios Loukas; wall paintings, early 10 cent, *in situ* Tokali Kilise, Goreme; 'Forty Martyrs' on wall painting, AD 963–969, *in situ* Dovecote Church, Cavusin; relief carving from Eskisehir, 9–10 cents, Archaeol. Mus., no. 755, Istanbul; *Commentaries of St. Gregory of Nazianzus*, c. AD 880, Bib. Nat., Ms. Gr. 510, Paris; *Psalter*, 9 cent, Mon. of the Pantocrator, Ms. 61, Mount Athos)

H2: Akritoi frontier cavalryman of an Anatolian theme, 9th century

In contrast to the elaborately equipped elite of Constantinople, the bulk of eastern *theme* horsemen seem to have been lightly armoured in felt or hardened leather, and to have fought as light cavalry. On his head is a protective *kamelaukion* of three layers of felt. His only body armour is a cloth-covered, thickly padded *kabadion* slit across the abdomen to enable the garment to bend when riding. Over his trousers he also has greaves of multi-layered felt. The large *epanoklibanion* cloak is dull grey, as recommended for camouflage during 'Shadowing Warfare'.

In addition to a small hardened leather shield with a pseudo-Arabic inscription he carries a single-edged proto-sabre, and a mace thrust into the breastband of his horse; Akritoi could also carry a lasso. The staining of a horse's mane, tail, hooves, etc., is mentioned in various poetic sources and later spread to eastern and central Europe. (Main sources: *Chludov Psalter*, c. AD 860, His. Mus., Ms. Add. Gr. 129, Moscow; *Psalter*, Byzantine late 9 cent, Bib. Nat., Cod. Gr. 923, Paris; icon painting, Byzantine 9–10 cents, St. Catherine's Monastery, Sinai; silver-plated mace from Tagance, 9–10 cents Russian or Byzantine, ex-Niederle; 'Forty Martyrs' on wall painting. Cappadocia AD 963–969, *in situ* Dovecote Church, Cavusin; 'St. Prokopis', late 10 cent mosaic, *in situ* Monastery of Hosios Loukas)

H3: Light infantry archer, 9th century

Infantry archers played a major role during the centuries when Byzantium was on the defensive but declined in importance when Byzantium expanded once again. They still appear in the art of the period, which showed them using large composite bows but generally lacking other arms or armour. Written sources also refer to the *solenarion*, which is now known to have been an arrow-guide identical to the Islamic *majra*. This man carries such a *solenarion*, and has a hypothetical additional pouch to his quiver to hold the short darts known to the Byzantines as *muiais* or 'mice'. His crude shield or mantlet is made of twigs, brambles and other available material as recommended in Byzantine military treatises. (Main sources: *Chludov Psalter*, c. AD 860, Hist. Mus., Ms. Add. Gr. 129, Moscow; wall paintings, Cappa-

Fortified palace at Khirbat at Baydah, east of the vast Safa lava plain of southern Syria. Although Roman in appearance, this large structure was built as a seasonal gathering place by the Ghassanid princes who served as Rome's powerful frontier allies. (Photograph by Père Antoine Poidebard)

docia 10–11 cents, *in situ* Bahattin Kilise, Peristrema valley; carved ivory box, Byzantine 10–11 cents, Dumbarton Oaks Coll., Washington)

INDEX

(References to illustrations are shown in **bold**. Plates are prefixed 'pl.' with commentary locators in brackets, e.g. 'pl. **E3** (42-43)')